MY BLUE YONDER

Carl Gamble

with Bob Rogers

*To Michael,
Live your dream and
fly.*

Carl Gamble

2-16-19

This book is a memoir. I have described events, locales, and conversations from my memories of them. In order to maintain their anonymity in some instances I may have changed the names of individuals and places, I may have changed some identifying characteristics and details such as physical properties, occupations and places of residence. Some names and identifying details have been changed to protect the privacy of individuals. I indicated in the text that other names were inserted to represent persons whose names I could not recall.

Dedication

To my dearly departed marvelous mother, Ora, for steadfast support and encouragement of my childhood dream to fly…

To my wife, Elaine, for everlasting love and devotion, especially when life was tough…

For my children…
Leilana
Davian
and grandchildren…
Jayli
John
Julian
Bianca

But they that wait upon the Lord shall renew their strength;
they shall mount up with wings as eagles;
they shall run, and not be weary;
and they shall walk, and not faint.

Isaiah 40:31King James Version (KJV)

Acknowledgements

This book was made possible by the great people around me who gave their time and talent to make it happen. Several years ago when I had the opportunity to see the excited reaction of middle schoolers to my talk about aviation careers, I was inspired to write my story in an effort to reach and inform more young people about possibilities for them in aviation. All I needed was an experienced collaborator and others to help me get my story in to print and into the hands of youth and the flying public.

During a Monday visit to my church, I met Bob Rogers, a man giving his time to teach computer courses to senior citizens. Bob had also published several historical books. First, we talked about our experiences in Vietnam. After hearing my story and purpose, Bob agreed to be my collaborator. I am truly grateful to Bob for guiding me with his knowledge and experience through this journey. In addition to writing with me, he was also the chief researcher and confirmed or corrected my memory of events and places. Speaking of memory, I am very grateful to my sister, Bobbie Gamble Hall, for helping me remember events from our childhood that had faded in my mind.

When Bob and I flew to Madison, Alabama, my hometown, I was pleasantly surprised by the number of childhood friends who turned out to greet us and reminisce about stories of the 1950s and 1960s. Thank you, Virgil Gilliam, Fernand Hammonds, Jack Jones, Roy Washington, Virgil Holman, Howard Miller, and William Moore.

I offer special thanks to schoolmate Virgil Gilliam and former Air Force pilots Nasif Majeed (C. J. Hayes), George Sledge, and Brian "Bee" Settles for giving their time and participating in extensive interviews. George and Brian are also retired airline pilots.

I am thankful for the late Tennessee State University Professor Cecil Ryan and the late Tuskegee Airman Alvon Johnson. Professor Ryan gave me my first flight instruction and let me know that once one has flown, it gets in the blood. Alvon Johnson, who finished pilot training in 1945 as World War II came to a close, gave me wise counsel and an aviator's friendship. When we were young captains in Vietnam, my classmate, General (Ret.) Lloyd "Fig" Newton shared valuable career information and feedback that further helped develop my perspective on aviation as a vocation. I am grateful for wise counsel from my friend and neighbor, the late Captain Cerea Beal, Jr., United Parcel Service pilot.

Many thanks are due Barbara Grainger for joining our team and providing her expert editing and structuring guidance that led to the successful completion of my book. I am very grateful to my wife, Elaine, for typing my reports of events so that Bob would not have to decipher my hand writing. As always, Elaine also gave me sage and common sense advice.

Many have made contributions to the success of my project and enriched my life. I am much obliged to each person named for their assistance. Though not named here, there are others who graciously contributed. They know who they are and what they gave. I want you to know, you have my undying gratitude.

I alone am responsible for any errors found herein.

Carl Gamble
Matthews, North Carolina
September 2016

Contents

Part One: Vietnam

Chapter 1:
A Burning Airplane

Clank! Ping! Ping! Crack!

"We're hit!" Master Sergeant McDonald sounded the alarm at the top of his baritone voice.

We were struck by a .50 caliber bullet ricocheting inside the frame of the fuselage and into the left wing and engine of our old "Gooney Bird." The projectile caused a fire in the left engine when it severed a fuel line. Master Sergeant John Thomas McDonald was my loadmaster. His friends called him "J. T."

We were flying at thirty-five-hundred feet over the Thu Bồn River in South Vietnam's Quảng Nam Province near the end of the dry season in 1969. At only one-hundred-twenty miles per hour, we were a sitting duck for a Viet Cong gunner spraying .50 caliber bullets. When we were hit, I was following the river and making a left turn toward the southeast over An Hoa, a village nestled in the river's curve. From our altitude, An Hoa, the emerald waters of the wide river, and the expanse of white sand between the two seemed tranquil–enemy antiaircraft fire, notwithstanding.

In my yoke and rudder pedals, I felt the vibration from the impact of the large caliber bullet when it struck. At first, I thought, *What the hell?* Anxiety caused involuntary squirming in my pilot's seat, expecting another hit. I glanced at the cockpit instruments and saw that my World War II era United States Air Force C-47D had remained in level flight. I thought, *Sturdy old bird. Thank God.* C-47s were used to transport troops and cargo during the big war against the Axis Powers–Germany, Italy, and Japan. It had occurred to me that some of these ancient, but solid, airplanes were older than me!

On the intercom, I said, "Sergeant McDonald, anybody hurt back there?"

"No, sir."

"Jim, Give me a damage report." Technical Sergeant James Hentz was my flight mechanic. On the ground, Jim supervised maintenance of our airplane. Aloft, he monitored several gauges from his usual position behind me and the copilot, including the vertical hydraulic bubble gauge mounted on the wall behind the copilot.

"Yes, sir." Jim turned and departed at a trot down the aisle.

My copilot, First Lieutenant Robert Coleman, or Bob as we called him, was making the same continuous scan of the instrument panel that I was making. In an emergency, neither of us could perform our duties and monitor the hydraulic fluid gauge. For that, we depended on Jim. Sometimes, though Jim was not Scottish, I thought of him as my 'Scotty', the engineering boss aboard the starship *Enterprise* in the television series, *Star Trek*.

Seconds later, I heard it. An unsynchronized dissonant sound came from the left engine, scarcely ten feet from my open side window.

With wide eyes, I turned my head to look. "Dammit! Bob, the left engine is on fire! Close the cowl flaps!" The controls for the cowl flaps were on the wall under the copilot's side window.

"Roger. Closing cowl flaps on the left."

JT's voice on the intercom interrupted my thoughts, "Sir, the left...."

"I see it!"

The panel instruments in our antediluvian craft showed no indication of trouble in either engine. Though we were sitting nearly elbow to elbow, I shouted, "Bob is the right engine still good?"

Bob, already looking out his side window, shouted back without turning his gaze away from the engine in the forward edge of the right wing. "It looks good, sir!"

I could hear relief in his voice. That was exactly what I was feeling. But, in less than a second, the feeling passed. Glancing again at the smoke trailing from the left engine and continuing to speak louder than ordinary, I told Bob, "I'm feathering the left. Check me."

For Tom, our navigator sitting behind the flight deck, my right hand must have been a blur. When learning to fly the C-47, I was told that in an emergency, a good pilot should in twenty seconds complete the procedure for shutting down a failing engine and beginning safe flight on the remaining engine. I had never completed the feat in less than twenty seconds. During training, no one mentioned what to do about an engine set ablaze by enemy action.

Sweating and barely breathing, I strained against the yoke with my left hand. I believe in fifteen seconds, with my right hand, I had changed the mix and pitch on the right engine, switched fuel tanks, shut off oil to the left, throttled it back, pressed the feather button, shut the fuel tank selector switch to the left, changed the mix on the right to emergency, closed the battery to the left, and discharged the left engine fire extinguisher.

Bob had grabbed the emergency checklist from its place above his head. When he looked up from reading and saw that I had finished the procedure, he said, "Damn. That was quick!"

"Yeah. Fire has a way of focusing the mind. Now, let's get the hell outta here!"

Under us, the Thu Bồn made a ninety degree turn to the southwest. I did not follow; instead, I kept my heading one-hundred-twenty degrees.

Bob showed a tentative smile, and then he frowned, "Do you mean bail?"

Suddenly, I remembered hearing the boys at the Danang Air Base Officer's Club say, "The Viet Cong in Quâng Nam Province don't play that 'rules o' war' shit. You ain't teachin' them a damn thing 'bout how to treat POWs. Why, they'll snatch your lil' Geneva Convention Card and nail the sucker to your fuckin' forehead." My friend, Bill Cobb, an old-school guy and seasoned F-4 pilot, offered up that profound truth and the boys agreed or sat like me listening with gaping eyes and slack jaws.

Though I had not thought of bailing out until Bob mentioned it, in about two seconds, I considered having the crew bail. I remembered telling my crew during every preflight briefing, "We will fly over hostile territory and there is a strong possibility we could be hit by enemy ground fire. If we're hit by enemy fire, or for another reason need to bail out, and I give the order to bail out; do so quickly. If you *think* you hear my order a second time, that will be an echo. Why? Because, I'll already be gone." Wow. Now I'm confronted with a decision that I never thought I'd have to make.

In one more second, I decided, "Oh, hell, no! We ain't bailing!"

Bob's nervous grin belied the tension. He was putting the checklist away and tried to make a joke. "By the way, sir, the checklist says you should see that the gear and flaps are up. I didn't see you check."

"Smart ass!" I grinned, and then grimaced. "Get on the horn. Declare an emergency and get us cleared for a 'straight-in' at Danang."

"What about the Marble Mountain airfield?"

"No. They can't foam the runway if we have to come in gear up." I looked again at the left engine. "Either that fire extinguisher didn't work or we've got one helluva fire. We need Danang!"

"Roger. Danang."

Bob broke into the radio traffic saying, "Mayday! Mayday! This is Paper Tiger Two-One!" Immediately, the drone of routine yammering on the radio quieted.

"Sir, I'll work out a new heading for Danang after your right turn." Tom spoke over my shoulder.

"No, Tom. I'm turning left. Forget the book. We're down to twenty-nine-hundred and dropping."

"But, sir, there's a…."

"I see that rocky-ass mountain dead ahead and I see it's higher than we are."

Close up, the mountain looked like a giant rock with trees growing out of cracks in its near vertical sides. And we were getting closer–quickly. My sweat poured. I thought, *so much for my bravado talk*. Though my knees trembled and my heart pounded, I forced myself to press more gently than usual on the left rudder pedal to begin what I hoped would be a slow and gradual turn toward Danang. With sweaty hands, I tightened my grip on the yoke and eased it counterclockwise. The airplane responded. I exhaled.

We cleared a lower mountain in the range by seven-hundred feet and flew past the big rocky mountain with less than a thousand feet between it and us. I thought, *God is always good*. I ended the turn on a new heading of three hundred fifty degrees.

The mountains of Cu Lao Cham Island in the South China Sea slid from my view out of the windshield as we came about with the horizon tilted. Looking, yet again, at the burning engine, I saw the confluence of the Rivers Vĩnh Điện and Thu Bồn beyond the left wing.

By now, we were well north and east of An Hoa. On my new heading, the Marble Mountains were in view to my right front and in the distance, beyond

Danang (aka "Rocket City), lay Monkey Mountain–or, Son Tra as locals called it. The tower responded using our radio call sign, "Paper Tiger Two-One, all traffic is holding. You're cleared for runway one-seven-Lima."

Bob looked at me. I was already shaking my head and saying, "Negative!" Bob nodded and responded to the tower, further explaining our emergency. I heard the tower say, "Paper Tiger Two-One, you're cleared 'straight-in' for runway three-five-Romeo."

Bob repeated, "Roger. Paper Tiger Two-One is cleared 'straight-in' for runway three-five-Romeo."

Smoke was pouring into the cockpit and cabin. I was blinking and squinting. My eyes were tearing and I could hear the crew coughing behind me. The farther I had gone into the turn, the more smoke entered the airplane. Our only exit from the airplane was behind the left wing. On that hot day, we flew our flying sauna without the door and with the cockpit windows full open. The temperature still felt like a hundred degrees inside the airplane. But now I closed my window because the smoke was obscuring my view of the instrument panel. The altimeter said we were descending through twenty-one-hundred feet. Now instead of mountains, below us lay the flat rice paddy laden Thu Bồn River delta, scarcely ten feet above sea level.

We were passing over Điện Bàn, when I said, "Tom, give me a heading from here to three-five-Romeo."

"Yes, sir."

9

Next, I heard rustling from Tom's map. "You're damned near on it. Come left ten."

"Roger. Left ten degrees."

Over my shoulder, I glanced to see Jim returning to his position. Panting, he said,

"Sir, besides the fire, that round must've busted a hydraulic line. I heard fluid sloshing under the floor." Jim's eyes were riveted on the hydraulic fluid gauge on the wall behind Bob as he continued his report. "Our fluid level is dropping rapidly. While I was aft, I could see from a window, fluid dripping from the trailing edge of the left wing."

No one spoke. For a long moment, the only sound was the right engine. Jim and Tom realized that Bob and I knew that losing hydraulic fluid meant soon we would have no way to control the flaps, lower the landing gear, or brakes–assuming we had landing gear down. In the heat of the cockpit, I felt a chill. Again, I thought, *Oh, shit!*

Our Mission that sunny Saturday afternoon, March 1, was to drop "Chieu Hoi" propaganda leaflets on the villages along the Thu Bồn River valley north and south of An Hoa, about twenty-five miles southwest of our home base at Danang. At takeoff, we had two tons of leaflets onboard, or about one million pages in fifty cardboard boxes. We could carry three tons. A chute was installed on the airplane to ease dropping leaflets. We called the leaflets bullshit. At first, I hated being called a 'bullshit bomber' pilot. However, long before today's mission, my one-hundred-eighty-second sortie in eight months, I had decided that it was not so bad an assignment after all.

Bob was talking again to the tower at Danang, but watching me.

I said, "Yeah, yeah. I know what the book said; 'don't turn in to the bad engine.' But I guess you see how fast we were losing altitude–and still are. There's no way we could make it back if we turned right for three hundred degrees, then left to align with three-five-Romeo. That'd take time we don't have."

In a shaky voice, Tom said, "And though I didn't see it at the time, we also would've had to clear a four-thousand-foot mountain."

"Damn! I didn't know that." I blinked and prayerfully reminded myself of God's goodness. Bob whistled and looked ashen. He nodded and continued talking with the tower.

I felt the usual movement of boxes in the cabin behind me as I fought to keep the airplane as near trim as possible. I thought Sergeant McDonald and crew, plus, the three army guys aboard for leisure and picture-taking, were continuing with the mission. Into the intercom, I said, "Sergeant McDonald, fuck the mission. We're trying to make Danang!"

"Yes, sir. We already quit. We stuffed the last loose paper down the chute. We're workin' the sealed boxes toward the door. We still have about a ton left. Sir, do I have your permission to ditch the bullshit?"

Relieved, I said, "Hell, yes! Ditch it. And quick!"

"Yes, sir!"

About six minutes had passed since we were hit. Heat from the fire on my left side was intense. My flight suit was sweat-soaked. Trying to clear my vision, I blinked repeatedly and flicked perspiration from my eyebrows with the backs of my hands. Drops of salty sweat on my aviator's sunglasses would have rendered them unusable on a big sky day.

Sputtering, Sergeant McDonald said, "S-s-sir, w-w-we can hardly breathe back here. Everybody is coughing. Can you get us on the ground soon?"

"Tell the guys to hang in there. We're closing on Danang. ETA: five minutes."

Actually, I only *hoped* we could make Danang in five minutes. Given our struggles at the time, and for all I knew, it could take ten or more minutes to reach Danang. And I had no idea if five minutes would be enough time to land *and* evacuate the airplane.

Watching the burning engine, I began slipping the airplane, keeping the nose to the left of our direction of travel. This was my attempt to prevent the fire from burning into the fuselage, only about four feet away from the auxiliary fuel tanks, and lessen the smoke pouring through the open door.

Pressure was building within me to avoid mistakes from which there would not be enough altitude to recover. We were down to twelve-hundred feet. A new set of worries popped into my head–landing. I thought, *What about the landing gear? Oh, my God, please don't let that tire burn.*

Two explosions inside the left wing in rapid succession challenged my control of the airplane.

Immediately, though I didn't think it could, the pucker factor increased. Bob stopped talking and stared at me, wide-eyed. Tom and Jim were quiet. I forgot the left landing gear and its tire housed in the same nacelle as the engine. I thought, *Oh shit. Is this the end?* Though we would have already been falling like a bowling ball without it, I looked over my shoulder to see if the left wing was still there. I shook my head at the irrationality of looking for the wing in spite of my flying experience and a degree in aviation technology. Aloud, I whispered, "Thank you, God."

Jim thumped the hydraulic fluid gauge with his finger nail and said, "Sir, I checked my watch when you announced our ETA three and a half minutes ago. If your estimated ETA is short by a minute or ninety seconds, my guess is this gauge will be bone dry."

Without looking back, I asked, "Is hydraulic fluid flammable?"

"No, sir. But it is combustible."

"What?"

Jim went on before I could interrupt. "Sir, the flash point for hydraulic fluid is about two hundred degrees. That means it won't be a hazard unless the engine fire spreads."

I soaked another sleeve wiping my brow, then took a deep breath and said, "Okay, guys. Listen up. Let me know whether I'm missing anything, but otherwise, here's what we'll do. Let's go in flaps up and save the hydraulic fluid for the brakes."

Bob frowned, "But, sir, what about the landing gear?"

"Pray for help from gravity when we let the gear down."

No one spoke.

I looked over my shoulder at Jim. He was still staring at the hydraulic gauge. "Jim, how's it looking?"

"Sir, the rate of fall in fluid level is looking worse for our ETA."

Even with the leftover ton of leaflets ditched, we were still losing altitude, though more slowly. Now, I figured some of my sweat was caused by second-guessing my decision not to bail and preparing for the landing. Again, I prayed, "*God, please help me get my crew and these men down safely. You already know what I want. Please don't let me die in this forsaken country. Please let me see Mama again, whom I love so dearly.*" I paused in my prayer to check our altitude. What I saw was not good. My heart raced. Matters looked grim.

While struggling to keep the airplane trimmed, I remembered a story Mama told me when I was I sixteen. She told her story only because I found her crying and asked why. For years, she had kept this story from me. Her husband shot and killed her brother in front of her when he was sixteen. I remembered that Mama did not let her brother's death destroy her life. Showing faith and courage, she had used the incident as an instrument to make herself stronger.

The tower interrupted my thoughts. An air traffic controller was telling us we were too low and would likely touch down short of the runway. "Can you go around?"

Without prompting, Bob broke protocol with his response. "Hell, no!"

I felt the tension in his voice.

The altimeter was unwinding through eight-hundred feet and we needed to fly for at least ninety more seconds. Without speaking, I discontinued slipping and aligned the airplane with our direction of flight.

With a wrinkled brow and an unsteady voice, Bob asked, "Sir, we should be higher, right?"

"Yes, dammit!" I didn't mean to sound testy. In my glance, Bob looked chastened. Immediately, I regretted my tone, but did not divert my attention from the parallel runways at Danang Air Base, now in sight. I could also see the fire trucks and emergency equipment Bob had requested. I said no more. I would try to remember to apologize later–if there was a "later." I followed the highway over the Cẩm Lê River Bridge, for it almost pointed to runway three-five-Romeo. Ahead, I could see the "T" intersection where the road ended a couple of hundred yards short of excavations for three large empty rectangular ponds at the end of the runway. The freshly turned earth was a rusty reddish-brown. On my previous one-hundred-eighty-one landings at Danang, the soil reminded me of my hometown; Madison, Alabama. Not today. My attention was riveted on the bold white threshold markings at the head of runway three-five-Romeo, not on the beauty one can observe from aloft.

Then it happened. I took a deep breath and repositioned my grip on the yoke. I felt better about our prospects. Now, I believed God and my mother's example of strength and courage would help me keep the crippled airplane flying long enough to reach the runway.

"Bob, set the right engine cowl flaps to trail."

"Roger. Setting right engine cowl flaps to trail."

On the intercom, I said, "Sergeant McDonald, we're in final approach. Buckle and brace for impact. Jim, you, too."

I heard Jim say, "Yes, sir." *Was that relief in his voice?*

Master Sergeant McDonald said matter-of-factly, "Roger, sir. Buckled and braced."

"Bob, grab your checklist. When we stop, we'll shut down the engine so the emergency crews can approach from both sides."

"Yes, sir."

Seconds later, we cleared by a few feet the last houses before reaching the runway. As we crossed the excavation, Bob instinctively reached to lower the gear. I said, "Not yet! On my command, let the gear down."

"Yes, sir!"

Bob said nothing further as he reflexively gripped his yoke showing white knuckles, and then released it as if he had grabbed the wrong end of a hot branding iron. Though it was Bob's turn to land the airplane, his movements confirmed he was more confident in a safe outcome with me landing the airplane. Secretly, I thought, *Well, shit, I'm not.* My faith wavered. I thought, *God, please don't leave me now.* My sweat poured. One by one, I wiped my hands on the legs of my flight suit below the knee and tightened my grip on my yoke.

Slowly, I raised the nose. I prayed, *God, please don't let this literally be my final approach.* Above the threshold markings and breathing again, I said, "Gear down!"

"Roger! Gear down!" The airplane shuddered. After a pause to look over his shoulder, Bob said, "Gear down and locked!"

We cleared the end of the runway about head-high–and I'm short.

"Roger." I glanced over my shoulder. After seeing the undamaged wheel of the left landing gear, I thought, *Thank God!* I said, "Gear down and intact!"

Two seconds later, at eighty-nine miles per hour, flaps up, and with me clenching my teeth and holding my breath again, we touched down with the left landing gear and the burning engine to the right of the center of the runway.

The tail-wheel on a C-47 is not retractable. I lowered the tail and said, "Tail-wheel down!"

Braking hard, I was vaguely aware of the fire wagons as they raced toward the place they thought we would stop. As we rolled to a stop, well short of the first ramp to a taxiway, I saw that I had avoided blocking the runway. I had no time to think about how to do it. It happened that the right engine pulled the airplane farther to the right. I applied the rudder before we stopped and guided the right landing gear off the runway and into the grass.

As Bob and I shut down the engine, I said, "Sergeant McDonald, get everybody out!" I had already heard feet scampering so I was not surprised that I heard no response from Sergeant McDonald.

About twelve seconds later, Bob and I were clawing to release our seat belts. "Let's get the hell out!" Now I realized that I was shouting so my voice would not betray the trembling in my body.

Tossing my headset aside, I motioned for Bob to squeeze through the narrow space between our seats, first. I went last to make sure everyone was out. I heard a helicopter at low altitude above our airplane, but could not focus on the question of why it was there. The smoke in the cabin was so thick that I could not see where I was going. Coughing and hacking, I crawled down the sloped floor toward the airplane's single exit. I did not see the doorless exit. When I reached the wall at the end of the floor, I thought, *this means all hands left safely.* That also meant I had missed the exit. I turned about and crawled, again, this time feeling for the exit on my left. Once I found it, I pivoted on my butt, swung my feet out, and jumped. On the ground, I felt the wind whipped by the wooden rotors of the HH-43 helicopter hovering above the airplane.

Now, I was afoot behind the burning left wing. My first thought was to turn and run as fast and as far from the airplane as my legs could carry me. The firefighters were spraying my crew. I gave a thumbs up to signal that I was okay. But they sprayed me anyway. The force from their hose against my chest knocked me down. I leapt to my feet and ran in place to avoid being knocked down again. With haste, the firefighters evacuated us away from our burning airplane.

I don't know how far we moved in the seconds before the fire reached the auxiliary fuel tank. Our old "Gooney Bird" exploded. I hit the dirt and turned to see the airplane enveloped in a huge fireball. Thick black smoke billowed skyward. The helicopter pilot's mastery of his rotor blades had kept the flames and smoke away from the door so my crew and our Army "passengers" could bolt from the airplane. The 38th Air Rescue Services' HH-43 helicopter, known as "Pedro," from Detachment 7 escaped the explosion and departed unharmed. I took all this to be a miracle.

Our three Army "passengers" gathered around and thanked me and my crew for a safe landing. The army guys swore no more sight-seeing, picture-taking flights. The bottom of my stomach fell as the thought occurred to me, *Double-check. Is everyone safe?* Holding my breath, I did a quick silent headcount. All were present. I took a deep breath.

Pushing stray blond strains from his eyes, Bob said, "Sir, your dazzling and distinguished flying saved the day! I'll fly with you anytime!" Not waiting for me to respond, Bob prattled on, "Tom, did you see me nearly screw up Carl's perfect landing by almost deploying the gear too soon?"

Tom said, "Yeah, and I heard Carl's quick correction. Wow! Carl, the turn you made in front of that mountain oughta be in a textbook."

Bob said, "Yeah, where are the film guys when you need 'em?"

Tom gestured with palms out and up, "How could you remain so calm?"

I said, "Humph! My flight suit was soaking-wet *before* we landed. I'm afraid all the sweating I did shows that I was the total opposite of cool. Calm? In fact, I'm still shaking. But thanks anyway."

The medics met us on the grass between runway 35R and the base's F-4 revetments. Fortunately, there were no life-threatening injuries–just bumps, bruises, and minor smoke inhalation. By now, my body was pumping less adrenalin and my knees were beginning to smart from crawling. No flight crew member opted to go to the hospital. None of the medics inquired about our mental condition, and I never gave a thought to the possibility of a wounded mind.

While their teammates sprayed foam on the burning airplane, a few members of the fire crew caught up to us while I was again mumbling my thanks to God for the miracle of a safe landing and the timely appearance of Pedro. I took another look at the destroyed airplane and found myself shaking my head. I thought, *To God be the glory*.

Gazing and visualizing what could have happened, I was jolted back to the present by the smell of fire retardant. The stench from the retardant was worse than a fish's toilet.

Chapter 2:
The Officer's Club

An airman threw a stone that made a loud clank against a steel dumpster behind the dining hall. Screeching cries of alarm, a flock of seagulls fluttered from their feast inside the open steel dumpster. Without formation, they circled above the street we traveled. Mingling with the sound of the seagulls was the roar of a flight of four propeller-driven bomb-laden A-1E Skyraider attack airplanes taking off in perfect two-by-two formations. For an instant, the planes, three blocks away, and the birds in the foreground were framed together in my passenger side of the jeep's windshield. The orderly flight of planes and the random directions of the white birds against the clear blue afternoon sky gave me another picture to remember from March 1, 1969. *Where was my camera when I needed it?*

The Air Rescue Service sergeant driving me back to my dormitory said, "Wow! Sir, did you see that?"

"I saw it. That was a great picture. The sight of the gulls and planes together made me forget for a moment the shit you fellas sprayed on me." I tugged at my wet flight suit. But only for a moment! How can you stand to have me in your jeep?"

"Well, sir. We handle it daily. So I suppose I've gotten used to it. Don't worry, sir. It'll wear off in time."

I turned in my seat and looked directly at my driver. "Until today, I'd never thought about how your firefighting buddies put out fires. That crap was wet, but it sure as hell ain't water. So what's in it making that powerful stench?"

The sergeant threw his head back and his laugh shook his belly. When he recovered, he said, "Sir, fluoroprotein foam is our primary weapon to knock down and smother aircraft fuel fires."

"Humph! The stink alone should knock down any fire!"

More laughter.

"Is the source of the stink some big-ass classified secret? I'm cleared for 'Top Secret.' Fluoride protein, or whatever the hell you said, didn't tell me what's in it."

Still laughing, he hacked and sputtered, "Sir, the protein in fluoroprotein foam is a mixture of soybeans, chicken beaks, fish bones, animal hooves, and horns combined with fluoro chemical surfactants and water."

* * *

In anxious anticipation of a hot shower, I hung my flight suit outside of my dormitory. I welcomed the thought that, unlike the crude hooches we lived in a few months back, there would be all the hot water I wanted in the new air-conditioned dormitory, with its stucco exterior and red roof. Wrapped in a towel at my waist, I nearly ran from my private room to the showers, in what I called the connector, for the building was shaped like an uppercase letter "H."

Remembering a four year old-television ad, I entered the shower. I could hear the announcer's voice in my head. "Every bar of Lifebouy Mint Refresher contains the essence of one hundred-twenty-five mint leaves. Soap has never smelled this good before, and neither have you."

After fifteen minutes, I smelled the same as before. I turned the water on again—hotter. Three scrubbing showers later and with irritated skin, I still smelled like a fish's toilet.

While pulling on a fresh flight suit, the first soap I knew came to mind. Mama made her soap from wood ashes, water, lye, and pig fat that she boiled in a large black iron pot over a fire pit in our backyard. The usual use of that pot was to boil water for washing clothes. Mama's soap.... I smiled at the thought, *is that what I need?* Calculating that it would soon be dawn back home in Madison, aloud, I said, "Mama, what will you do today?"

* * *

Scenes of the scramble to escape the burning airplane would not leave my mind. What if we had been seconds slower crawling out? What if I had turned right? What if the left engine fuel shutoff valve had leaked? In my head, the Kodak Super-8 video of the final explosion on the ground had me and the crew still inside. It played on an uninterrupted loop. I could not find the stop button on that piece of video; nor, could I erase it.

Trying anything to distract my mind, I focused on home–Alabama. Sitting on the edge of my bed with my hands at the sides of my head and my elbows resting on my thighs, memories of long-ago days in Madison returned. I closed my eyes and saw the swift movement of Mama's fingers picking cotton fiber cleanly from the bolls and shoving handfuls into the long sack slung over her shoulder and being dragged behind her. The rows seemed miles long and ended at the woods. Barely taller than an Alabama cotton stalk, I always started in a row next to her, but couldn't keep pace. Mama picked two rows on each pass through the field. In the fall of 1950, cotton was the central thought on the minds of Madison's less than six hundred residents.

Meanwhile, on the other side of the globe that September, C-47s were hauling troops and supplies from Japan to Korea in yet another war.

Picking cotton was back-bending and backbreaking work that lasted from sunup until sundown. We needed the money for food and clothing. So, at age seven, I helped as best I could. My meager pickings were added to Mama's at the end of the day, and she'd collect our small earnings. Less and less frequently, I complained about my back hurting. I knew Mama would gently scoff and laugh. She would tell me, "It can't be your back. Young'uns your age don't have backs; only gristle. And I know for a fact that gristles don't hurt."

We lived in a small frame house on Pension Row. Pension Row was founded by former black Civil War soldiers given pensions by the federal government. The "Row," our center of commerce and residence, was located two blocks west of the tiny downtown area run by Madison's whites. From the "Row," as dawn broke, we made our way to the fields. Since it was September, my schoolmates and I should have been in classes. That was not so in the rural south for many black children. For cotton-belt black children, summer vacation ended soon after Independence Day. But school shut down again for the work of gathering the cotton crop by late August and remained closed until early October.

My best friend, Virgil, and I walked to school together as white children rode past us in buses. And as worse luck would have it, during my first-grade year, our elementary school was destroyed by fire. Education for me, Virgil, and neighborhood children continued in black churches that were small white frame structures not far from the "Row." Each church housed students in two grades until a new school was built four years later. When Virgil and I were promoted to second grade, we merely crossed the aisle and sat in pews on the other side of the same church.

The same hated OshKosh B'gosh overalls and plaid flannel shirts served me as school attire and in the cotton fields. Virgil dressed the same as I and except for picking cotton in different fields, we did almost everything together. Virgil was bigger than I. With his size, Virgil helped me in fights that I started before the boys wearing nice waist pants, held up by stylish and colorful rubber galluses, could begin hazing me; for I was short and skinny. I hated being little as much as I hated overalls. Sometimes, I wore two pairs of boxer shorts to seem bigger.

Though I was taught not to listen to old folks' conversation, I played at the edge of earshot and pretended not to hear. I found what adults had to say fascinating and bewildering. When they gathered to pass the time, I made it my business to listen. In the warm evenings of late September, sitting in the dark on the front porch, Mama and her neighborhood friends would swat mosquitoes and lament.

Mama said, "Them radio news people claim the recession ended 'bout this time last year."

Her friend from across the street, Miss Mildred, said, "Chile, they sho' ain't talkin' 'bout no Alabama. Did it end fer any o' y'all, yet?"

Laughter.

Old Uncle George, from down the Row, who was nobody's uncle that I remember, said, "Naw. I'm heah to tell ya, I's sho' glad today's Sadday and the last day of the mont' to boot. 'Cause I ain't felt de end o' nothing, 'cep my lil' change runnin' out 'fore time."

More laughter.

Uncle George continued. "'Sides, yisdiddy dem same radio folks said the price for a pound o' cotton done jumped up leb'n cents all the way to forty cents."

Mama said, "Humph! Any y'all seen wages jump up for pickers? Last I seed, we still gettin' a measly three copper Lincolns a pound."

Miss Mildred, said, "Yeah, our wages gone jump up alright–on a cold day in hell!"

Raucous laughter.

As the laughter died, Uncle George stood, stretched, held his battered felt hat aloft while rubbing his shiny bald spot, and said, "Y'all may soon hafta fine som' else to grouse 'bout."

Miss Mildred said, "'Scuse me. Come agin."

"How cum y'all ain't talkin' 'bout whatcha gone do atter that new fangl' cottonpickin' machine takes away our lil' jobs?"

Mama put her hand over her mouth. I heard alarm and fear in her voice. "George, you don't mean to tell me that it's true what they say on the radio 'bout that new machine; you know that the thing actually works and all."

"'Fraid so, Ora. Big white farmers is buyin'em this year from that new International Harvester comp'ny right over there in Memphis."

Hands akimbo, Miss Mildred said, "They's already got the cotton gin. Looks like we's gone be put plum outta any kinda work to do wid cotton."

Then there was a pause. Now, Uncle George broke the silence. "Well, this thing is real enouf and it's a comin'. Why, anutter comp'ny's gone be make'em right down the road there in Gadsden."

By her voice, I knew Mama had not recovered from the thought of being replaced by a machine. I was still trying to figure out how a machine could pick cotton. Resigned, Mama said, "You mean right here in Alabama?"

"Yessum."

"Do, Lawd!"

The quiet was palpable.

Long minutes went by before Uncle George cleared his throat and said, "Sometimes, there's happy news from the radio. The Brooklyn Dodgers done beat dem ol' Phillies this afternoon, 7-3."

A cheer went up from those assembled. Even as a child, I sensed that they were happy to change the subject. I know I was, for I knew from where money came for living expenses.

Uncle George's friend, Mr. Jimmy, turned perky. He said, "Yeah, and if'n they win tomorrow, the season'll end in a flat-footed tie 'twix dem and those damned Phillies!"

Mama asked, "Did Jackie hit a home run?"

"Naw. But ol' Roy did. And, that Duke fella did, too. George, who's pitching tomorrow?"

"Don Newcombe."

* * *

Shortly before happy hour, I arrived at the Officers Club still reeking despite of a half-hour shower, scrubbing my skin raw, and applying deodorant, copious splashes of after shave lotion, and cologne. Marvin Gaye's soulful rendition of "I heard it on the grapevine" was playing on the Wurlitzer and the usual blue haze from cigarette and cigar smoke hung in the air.

"Hey, Carl! Today, your money ain't no good in heah. 'Cause right now, you're the man of the hour." That was Bill Cobb rising from the chair he had sat on backward and heading to greet me, grinning. Other pilots were rising to follow him. Bill was the only person wearing sunglasses inside the club. That was a part of his image. Bill was the coolest pilot ever. He was wearing sharkskin slacks, a silk shirt and matching silk socks, and the finest shoes in the room. Everyone else was wearing the usual flight suit or fatigues and boots.

Bill reached me first with his hand extended. "Man, we just got the big news that you landed a burning plane this afternoon."

As he shook my hand, Bill's expression changed as if I had slapped his face. His nostrils flared. He released my hand and backed away, letting others approach me. Alex Dawson said, "Every one of us thinks you're one brave pilot." But, Alex, too, let his expression drop and quickly stepped back. Alex's hand flew toward his nose, but with discretion, he diverted his hand to rub down his face as if he had a Van Dike goatee and let it drop from his chin. From a growing distance, Bee Settles said, "Brother Man, yes, it's sure enough true that you're a hero, but you're also lucky to be alive."

Their body language said, "Let me give you a hug." But all backed away, stumbling over each other.

Then Bill said what no one else would say, "Man, we know you had a butt tightening ordeal out there today, but did you shower? You smell like shit."

Wide-eyed, they were gazing at my mouth, waiting for words as if they would see them drop from my lips. Indignant, I said, "Hell, yes. I showered for a half hour and scrubbed my skin raw trying to get rid of this damn smell."

Bill's hands flew akimbo. With his cigarette dangling from his lips, he demanded, "Well, what the fuck kind of stink won't wash off?"

After a quick explanation of fluoroprotein foam, we settled at two tables, five friends at one and me alone at another, but within earshot. Following Bill, friends delivered round after round of Jack Daniels to my table as they asked for the details of my harrowing flight–bringing back to my mind exactly what I was trying to forget.

Bob Coleman, my copilot, followed a group of his friends into the club. When he spotted me, he laughed and said, "Hey, fearless leader. I know why you have that table all alone."

I yelled back, "Yeah, tonight we're two of a kind. I'll bet you'll have a table of your own, too."

He approached my friends' table, but stopped short. "Let me tell y'all from over here, 'cause I smell like Carl. Y'all can write home and tell the folks at Tennessee State that Carl is one helluva pilot. I guess everybody at Danang Air Base knows the end of today's headline story. But wait–there's more. Take it from a guy who was there. To save our lives, Carl made lightning decisions, one after another, that minimized the fire, limited the smoke pouring in on us, and without, put us on a heading for home. On final approach, we were coming in low. I want you know he had the balls to *not* deploy flaps or landing gear until we were only about five feet above the runway!" To demonstrate, Bob held his hand about shoulder high. "So lemme tell y'all. Add Carl's flying skills atop that cool decision making, and what you have is a perfect and safe touchdown—and a damn thankful crew. Now, you know the rest of the story."

Bill turned toward me wearing his infrequent solemn and serious face. "Damn, Bro. We knew you were a brave man 'cause you landed that flaming wreck. But, Carl, you didn't tell us these details. Man, what you did oughta be taught to every rookie. Dude, if this ain't fuckin' Silver Star shit; grits ain't grocery."

I shrugged and fidgeted with a glass in front of me.

From my friends rose a chorus of 'Amens' and 'Well dones'. I felt warm and embarrassed.

After more good-natured banter, Bob returned as near as he could to his friends. You see, though there was no rule in the club about seating, blacks and whites usually sat in separate groups.

The club had no waiters. Led by Bill, we entered the line to pick up steaks that we would grill outside of the club. A major in front of Captain Bill Cobb turned and said, "Why do you always wear those sunglasses in here?"

Bill didn't miss a beat. He raised his chin and looked the major in the eye and said, "You listen here, muthafucka. These are *my* damn shades. I'll wear'em anytime and anyplace I damn well please."

Without turning heads, the eyes of black and white officers shifted from side to side to surreptitiously gauge reactions of comrades of their respective races. The silence in the room was palpable.

The crimson-faced major's blond hair flew as he snapped his head around and focused on a steak.

Long after dinner and more drinks than I can remember, I could not walk. At some time that night, another friend from our years together at Tennessee State, Lloyd "Fig" Newton, had the courage to overcome my stink. Over a distance roughly the length of a football field, Fig ferried all one-hundred twenty pounds of me on his back to my dormitory.

Chapter 3:
Back in the Saddle

"Halt, turkey! Stay where you are." That was a laughing Bill Cobb yelling from his table. We were back at the club, our usual haunt. Bill was seated between two of my grinning fellow Tennessee State alum friends, Chuck Guthrie and Lorenzo Pugh. Like Bill, both were F-4 pilots.

Bill pointed and said, "Sit over there." After a pause, he added, "Humph. You don't look too good."

In my best sarcastic voice, I said, "Good morning to you, too."

"We missed yo' lil' turkey ass in the bunker last night."

Chuck elbowed Bill and said, "After his heroics, didn't we promote Carl to 'eagle?' Man, show some respect."

"Oh, yeah, I forgot. Sorry. Anyway, I heard Bee tell you that yo' ass was lucky. But, if I were you, I wouldn't try to stretch my lil' luck. Next time, it might be 'Charlie' who's lucky enough to send a fuckin' rocket into our dorm and *yo'* lil' eagle luck jes might be at an end."

Chuck and Pugh laughed.

Perplexed and frowning, I said. "What the hell are y'all talking about?"

Chuck said, "Bill's just giving you some good advice. Take it. Get to the bunker next time the rockets hit us."

I could feel my face fall and shoulders droop. A rocket attack! And I slept through it. I slumped onto a chair two tables away from the boys. I said, "I dreamt there was a rocket attack last night. It sounded real."

Bill laughed and pounded the table with his fist. "Now, I've heard loads of bullshit in my time, but that damn weak-ass tale of yours takes the cake." Then he pointed at me and without even a hint of a smile he said, "Boy, next time you'd best get yo' lil' narrow ass in a bunker."

I sat holding the sides of my head, elbows on my table. I felt weak and dizzy at the realization that a rocket could have been my end hours ago. ...*live through landing a burning plane to expose myself to rocket fire before dawn the next day...* Deeply troubled, under my breath, I muttered, "What's wrong with me?"

Bill spoke again. "By the way, turkey, oops, I mean eagle. It ain't morning anymore. It's a quarter past one."

* * *

Many days after landing the burning plane, the video tape in my mind of my near-disaster was still playing on a continuous loop. Tuesday of the next week was another hot day, and for me, a day of deep thought. Unable to sleep that evening, I sat outside my dormitory nursing a beer in the faint silver light of a waning moon, enjoying a gentle sea breeze off the South China Sea. The sounds of a busy airport surrounded me. *Why am I here? How did I get from Madison to Danang, a place I never heard of before, a place where I came within seconds of dying?*

The word 'dying' stopped my video. My mind went back to flight school at Laughlin Air Force Base, not far from the confluence of the Rio Grande and the Pecos River, in southwest Texas, and a classmate known as Rex. Robert Alan Rex, unlike most of us newly minted officers, was married and completely serious about his studies and career. He was a reservist, who had returned to school, earned a bachelor's degree, and entered Officer Training School. Though we were not buddies, my memory of him had not faded, for his diligence earned him the number one position in our class and the Outstanding Pilot Award. The scuttlebutt was that he had earlier been named Outstanding Senior Student at Brigham Young University. Here was a guy to emulate.

Two months after I arrived at Danang, Rex deployed to Thailand, to fly F-105D fighter-bombers. I shook my head at the memory of seeing his name on the *Air Force Times*'s "Missing In Action" list in December. Everyone knew that he was gone. His body had not been recovered because the crash site was in territory held by the enemy. A Forward Air Controller flying near Rex's target in Laos around noon that sunny day reported that Rex's plane, in a flight of four F-105s, did not come out of a sixty degree dive and that his canopy was still in place on impact.

In my fist, I crushed my empty beer can. What of Rex's wife and daughter? What was to be gained in place of their loss? How might our country have benefited from the likes of a studious hardworking diligent Robert Alan Rex living his life and raising a family in his native Utah? Or, others like him? Rex was one of our best and brightest. What a waste... Now, more than ever, my question is still, what am I doing here?

My tape hit the start button.

* * *

Complying with my squadron commander's "request" for an incident report was not a problem, for I remembered far too much detail about my last flight. On the other hand, it *was* a problem, because it sharpened the images on my internal movie reel. The more I relived the experience, the less ready I was to fly again.

Days were passing and I was continuing to say to my commanding officer, "Sir, I'm just not ready to fly, yet. I'm still trying to get my head around how close I came to dying in an unarmed low flying slow-ass airplane."

My CO rubbed his chin and appeared for a time to be in deep thought. Finally, he said, "Look. Carl, why don't you take some time off and clear your head?"

Surprised, I said, "Sir?"

"Yes. I'm serious. Be creative. Start with some local outings around Danang. Then, let's think bigger.

I'll look into another out-of-country R&R, or ferrying aircraft to maintenance in Taipei."

That got my attention. Smiling, I said, "Sir, do you have all the electronics and cameras you want from Hong Kong?"

He laughed and said, "Come to think of it, I do need a few items. I'll bet others might want to give you a shopping list, too. So, go ahead. Add Hong Kong to your list."

Grinning, I said, "Yes, sir!"

"In the meantime, I want you to know that you're one of my best pilots. I'm sure you won't be surprised that you'll be getting the Distinguished Flying Cross for saving the crew and passengers."

I suppose surprise was written on my face.

He went on to say, "Actually, I think since the plane was destroyed by enemy action and you saved all aboard, you should get a Silver Star." He shrugged. "But, the old man decided on the DFC and an Oak Leaf Cluster for another Air Medal."

"Sir, the Silver Star doesn't matter to me. What does matter is that I still have my life."

My CO blinked and his expression changed. Slowly nodding, he said, "Carl, I admire your humility." He stood and continued. "Well, right now, I'm taking you off the flight schedule for a while. But understand I'm going to need you back for duty as soon as possible."

* * *

Several days later, I took a morning stroll along the gleaming white sands of Danang's oceanfront, known to G.I.'s as China Beach or My Khe, as the locals called it. There, I met a marine corporal recovering from a battle wound. He sat with me and my driver at a very American picnic table in the shade of palms and short cypress-like trees I had never seen before. The bottom four feet of each tree growing out of the sandy soil was painted white. We were surrounded by airmen, marines, sailors, and soldiers at other picnic tables–all enjoying another day of well-earned R&R at the beach. This in-country R&R center was a part of the United States Marine Corps compound known as the Marble Mountain Air Facility and was located on a prime beach.

For a long while after an initial greeting, we sat in silence, watching shirtless men in fatigues and boots play catch with a softball and oversized mitts. Most wore swim trunks. Some passed an American football back and forth on the water's edge, while others dug starfish out of the wet sand, took photos, caught waves on surf boards, or cruised in power boats. At one of the 'official concessionaires' that looked a lot like a walkup Dairy Queen, I bought beers for my tablemates.

For a time, the sights took my mind off matters that I wanted desperately to avoid. But too soon, my nemesis drifted back. To push it out of mind, I said to the marine, "Are any of your buddies here on R&R with you?"

The corporal took a sip of his beer and said, "No, sir. It's just me. I'm nearing the end of my recuperation at the Naval Hospital across the highway—over there." He pointed west through the trees. "My battalion's up near Quảng Tri City. Where're you fellas from?"

"Danang Air Base. About four straight-line clicks west of your hospital. What happened to you?"

"Oh, in a fire fight, I caught an AK round. Damned thing passed through the fleshy part of my arm, right here below the elbow." He touched his left arm. "But, it's all better now."

"Are you going home?"

He laughed a cruel laugh and said, "Oh, hell no, sir. They're sendin' my ass right back to Quảng Tri in a matter of days."

The corporal was quiet. Rubbing my chin, I reflected on how lucky—actually, how blessed I was. I didn't have a scratch on me, save for my bruised knees. He had an enemy inflicted bullet wound. I studied his face and saw that, at least outwardly, he had accepted that he was on his way back to more danger, combat, the bush, and primitive living. Perhaps, and most likely, he's not willing to go. But go, he will. That's what we do; when duty calls, we salute smartly and go in harm's way.

After lunch, I will be on my way back to my dormitory and air conditioned comfort. I felt guilty of something I could not yet identify—but what? It nagged at me. The answer seemed close at hand, but still eluded me—it was that close, alas, just beyond reach....

Then it hit me. My war was the same as the corporal's, yet different. It was all there in the "b's" bayonets, bullets, bombs, and bullshit. My war was really a delivery service. So was Cobb's. Directly to the enemy, I delivered bullshit; Cobb delivered bombs. Unlike the quiet corporal, we didn't see individual enemy soldiers, much less fix bayonets and personally confront an enemy eye-to-eye who was determined to kill you before you could kill him. Yet, my war and Cobb's war supported the same American national policy as the corporal's war. That policy still made no sense to me.

Like Cobb, I will renew my determination not to die in this God-forsaken country.

* * *

"Why don't you try poker? Now, there's a game where paying attention is a must. It'll for certain make you focus, or you'll soon be broke." Alex laughed and continued shuffling a deck.

Picking up the dice from the table under Alex's hands, I said, "Poker looks like a longer learning curve than dice. Am I right?"

Alex twisted his mouth in a frown and then said, "Hmm. I don't know. The stuff you'll need to learn may be different, but could take close to the same amount of time."

"Huh? What's to learn? How many different ways are there to throw dice?"

Alex threw his head back in a hearty laugh. "That's what I mean. You shoot dice; you do not throw dice." Momentarily, he said, "In two words, you need to know 'etiquette and language.'"

"What?"

"You heard me, turkey. Oh, that's right you're an eagle, now. Humph. I think turkey sounds better. Always did. Always will. Who the hell's going to laugh at an eagle?"

In spite of myself, I laughed with Alex.

We were sitting at a table near the center of the club. Alex took the dice from me and began my first craps lesson. He held up a small white cube and said, "You will hear some call this a 'die' and a pair, 'dice.' Others call either one or two by the same word– 'dice'…"

My friend, Jack Daniels, was failing me. Jack had been my close companion and nurse for many days and nights at the club–for free. The boys were still buying drinks for me. The smell of fluoroprotein foam had worn away, but my video tape had not faded at all–no matter whether I was stone sober or inebriated. I had come to understand Jack's sedation limitations. Further, Jack could not stop my video, nor did he help me determine if I was as tough as I thought I was from the fights I started at elementary school, or what was now keeping me out of the cockpit. Jack offered no answers and was a rapidly diminishing temporary distraction.

After learning some craps stuff from 'snake eyes' to 'boxcars' to 'pass/don't pass bets;' I found out that Jack also helped me lose money–fast. When Jack was "helping me" I was so bad at craps that several mornings, Bee would stop by my room and put money in my hand.

The first morning, I said, "G'moanin', Bee. What's this for?"

"That's the money I took from your pockets last night before you could lose it shootin' craps–or, tryin' to shoot." He grinned and walked away while I gaped at the money in my hand.

* * *

By Saturday night of the next week, I decided I needed real help. Sometime after midnight, I awoke in a sweat from a dream–my weekly nightmare. In the dream, *I had landed and brought the burning airplane to a stop on the runway. As I scampered out of the captain's seat of my C-47, an explosion ripped through the left wing. The blast hurled me against the right sidewall of the fuselage and I slid to all-fours. I felt an oily liquid on my fingers. There was a violent "whoosh" and my hands and flight suit were set alight. In a blinding flash, the auxiliary fuel tank detonated and added to the ensuing conflagration. My screams mingled with those of my crew in agony from our burning flesh. All of us perished in a billowing firestorm.* As usual, I awoke in a panic and bolted upright in bed. I frantically rubbed my hands. My breathing and heart rate slowed when I realized that my hands were fine and that it was only a dream– again. I sat alone in the darkness as my troubled mind gradually downshifted to near normal.

The following morning, Sunday, still hung over, I stood in front of the base chapel. Mass goers streamed from the building and filed past me on both sides.

As the sea gull flies, the chapel may have been as close as half a football field to my dorm. Looking up at the soaring A-line roof, I was reminded of the photographs I had seen of the recently completed United States Air Force Academy Cadet Chapel. My base chapel did not have seventeen spires like the academy's chapel, but the modern architecture of the roof line also reminded me of a delta-winged F-106 Delta Dart in vertical flight. And, instead of the gleaming aluminum tetrahedrons of the academy chapel, the roof of Danang's chapel was supported by rows of large square wooden beams that formed isosceles triangles if one included the ground as their base. The same thick beams extended below the top of the exterior walls all the way to the ground as flying buttresses. The entire structure was a soothing brown, reminiscent of African mahogany.

Inside, I craned my neck to follow the vertex of the high ceiling from the front door to the opposite end of the chapel. The interior color was the same brown as the exterior.

A Catholic chaplain startled me. "Good morning, captain." He was cheerful. Moving past me, he read my name tag. He said, "Captain Gamble, may I help you in some way?"

I thought, *I can read a name tag, too*. I focused and spoke slowly. I was determined to pronounce ending "g's" and avoid slurring my words. "Good morning, Chaplain Balducci. I'm just looking for a quiet place to think." As an afterthought, I added, "And pray."

Though I was nearly an hour early for protestant services, Chaplain Balducci left me with my thoughts and prayers on the first pew. I bowed my head before the altar and thanked God again for my life. I repeated the 'Lord's Prayer' several times. And then, I prayed, *Almighty God, I need big help. Please guide me out of my web of tangled thoughts. Thank You again for delivering me physically from the plane. Now, please deliver me from my nightmares and my mind's movie reel repeating falsely that all perished at flight's end. Please grant me guidance. Thank You for Your divine deliverance. Amen.*

Chaplain Bates noticed that I did not leave my pew at the close of the Protestant service and sat beside me. His voice was warm and kind. He said, "Son, do you want to talk about it?"

Was the guidance I prayed for forthcoming already? "Yes, sir."

An hour passed quickly. When Chaplain Bates had heard my story, he said, "Captain Gamble, it has been my pleasure to meet you. Your reputation as a pilot has preceded you. What you accomplished, in the face of great danger, was extraordinary. I salute your courage and skill."

"Thank you, Major Bates, sir."

"Son, hold your head up. Even men of courage have a natural reaction to danger. If a man tells you that he never has fear, he's lying. Our brains are wired for survival above all else. You've, no doubt, heard of 'fight or flight', yes?"

"Yes, sir."

"Well, that applies to brave pilots, too. I think imagining what would have happened had you not escaped the plane once on the ground is something I would do, too. Your dreams further complicate your state of mind. My guess is, in time, you'll get past what *could* have happened, but, by God's grace, *didn't* happen.

"This brings to mind a baseball story we can discuss now and a football story I'll tell you later. When both of us were lads, Ted Williams landed a burning plane during the Korean War.

I frowned. "Do you mean the Boston Red Sox slugger?'

"Yes, he is the very same. Though Ted had no passengers, he may have had the same thoughts as you."

"How long before he flew again?"

"Ted flew the next day. Come by and see me during the week and let's talk again."

"Yes, sir. Thank you very much."

Leaving Chaplain Bates, I felt hopeful. His words about Ted Williams reminded me of a forgotten conversation from a warm fall Saturday afternoon among men sitting on wooden milk and Coca-Cola crates under a dome-shaped chinaberry tree next to Mr. Archie's store in Madison. Weeks later, John F. Kennedy would be elected president. In the fading sunlight, Uncle George and his friend, Mr. Jimmy, played checkers on a homemade board resting on an upside down milk crate. They were engaged in their usual heated arguments about baseball and war, with the men sitting around them waiting for a turn on the board.

Uncle George said, "I'ma tell ya agin. War messes a man up on the inside. He might, then agin, he might not have scars on the outside. Ya won't never see the scars I'm talkin' 'bout–'cause they be inside."

Someone said, "Aw, how can a man have a scar nobody kin see?"

Mr. Jimmy said, "Listen to George. Y'all know he fit in World War One–back when they called it 'shell-shocked.' He done been whar y'all ain't and best hope to never go. Nigh, George, he a fine Christian man and ain't gone say but so much."

Mr. Jimmy held a checker piece, which was a soda bottle cap, between his fingers as he pointed in the man's face. "Lemme tell y'all muthafuckas straight from the shoulder. George, always talk right nice in his Christian way. What he meant was what a man sees in war fucks wid a man's mind. In my war, 'WW2,' dey called it 'battle fatigue.' Could be, a fella saw his best buddy wid'im in same foxhole hit in the face wid a damn big ass piece o' hot shrapnel and lose half his head. The man *not* hit could be all fucked up inside from seein' his buddy's life knocked outta'im in a damn instant. Would he think it coulda been him? You damn right! He'll think for years, 'Muthafucka, dat shit coulda kilt me 'stead o' him.' Nigh on top a dat, he still grievin' de loss o' his friend. You sombitches dat ain't never been no whar but Madison County oughta keep ya damn moufs off'n whatcha don't know nothin' 'bout."

The man said, "Is that what you saw?"

Mr. Jimmy's nostrils flared. He leapt from his seat and the bottle cap checker pieces went askew. Ignoring the sliding bottle caps, Uncle George made up and down motions with his hands. "Now, Jimmy, jes calm down and rest yo' feets. He ain't knowed not to ask old soljers lak us 'bout what we done seed. But, I will say this much 'bout it. Jes lak outside scars, inside scars be de same way. Everybody don't get'em. Won't call no names from here 'bouts, but jes look at dese two fine ball players. Atter Korea, Bobby Brown returned to the Yankees a shadow of his ol' self. I don't know what dat boy saw, but war did'im no good. Now, take dat Ted Williams, he landed a burning plane in Korea dat done been hit by enemy fire. But I bet the Red Sox wuz sho' happy ol' Ted came back playin' lak he wuz tryin' a make up for lost time. Why, don't you know, ol' Ted jes finished up his playin' days wid a homer in his last at bat! Lak I said, some get scarred; some don't."

* * *

In the Twenty-first Century, the United States Department of Health and Human Services' National Institute of Mental Health (NIMH) uses the term "Post Traumatic Stress Disorder, or PTSD" for what Uncle George and Mr. Jimmy called "shell-shocked" and "battle fatigue." NIMH lists the number one symptom of PTSD as "flashbacks–reliving the trauma over and over."

* * *

A few days later, I made my first arrival in Hong Kong as the copilot of an Air Force C-47 we were ferrying from Nha Trang to Taipei for maintenance. This was also my first time back in the cockpit and we flew over twenty-five hundred miles in seven days. In my pockets were shopping lists from my CO and several of the boys for electronics and cameras. I was looking forward to three days in Hong Kong before our onward journey to Taipei.

During final approach at Hong Kong, my pilot made a sudden sharp and surprising turn while descending from an altitude of less than six hundred feet. Involuntarily, I held my breath. My heart pounded until I saw his calm demeanor and heard his responses to the tower in an unexcited voice. So, I exhaled. At first, it felt like we were maneuvering for a place in Kowloon's street traffic. We were at the end of over five hours in the cockpit and cruising at about 150 miles per hour in an uneventful flight–so far.

On the ground, I learned that the low altitude forty-seven degree right turn over Western Kowloon to land on Kai Tak Airport's runway 13 was necessary and the stuff of legend. I had no idea that when the turn was completed, the plane's altitude was to be only one hundred forty feet! I was told that veteran pilots called it the 'Hong Kong Turn' and passengers called it the

Kai Tak Heart Attack.' I thought, *How can 'fight or flight' apply here? Hmm…flight…?*

The chief attraction for me at the airport was the presence of the many Boeing 707s sporting the logos and colors of the world's major airlines. I smiled at the memory of having been offered and taking the controls of an airborne KC-135, the 707's near twin, when I was in Air Force ROTC Summer Camp. After the Aircraft Commander directed me to make several turns, he told me my flying performance revealed excellent skills. *Perhaps, someday I'll fly one of these babies.* The talk I had with Chaplain Bates and my periods of introspection alone in my dorm room helped turn my attention to connecting my past with a future. This felt useful, though, from time to time, the flaming images and dreams returned. The 707s were a reason to connect the future to my tangled web of thoughts. Those sleek 707s hit the pause button on my video tape.

* * *

It was like television. At a Kowloon night club, the proprietor marched them in like the lineups I remember from the TV series, *Dragnet*. When the line stopped, just like on *Dragnet*, he had them turn and face the men waiting to identify their choice. They were not burglary or murder suspects. They were attractive young women who were 'owned' by the proprietor of the club. By taste and fancy, a man could choose one of the women as his escort for an evening of drinks, chat, and sex–all for a price paid to her "owner."

During my second visit to this Kowloon club, which was only two white-roofed red Mercedes taxis and a big green and white double decker ferry ride away from my hotel in central Hong Kong, I met a marine sergeant who was in his last evening of R&R. I first saw him through the blue haze of cigarette smoke hanging in the air. His long face and contemplative mood caught my attention.

I stood by his table and said, "You look like a fella in exactly what I'm avoidin'–deep thought."

The marine stopped stirring the dregs of his drink, took a long look at me, and above the music said, "You look like a pretty serious fella yourself." He pushed a chair toward me. "Join me. We can drown our deep thoughts together."

I grinned. "Drownin'em sounds good. And while we're at it, let's weight'em and sink'em deep. Lemme buy you a drink."

He displayed a fleeting smile. "Thank you."

(I do not remember his name. So I will call him Ken.)

In a short time, my new acquaintance, Marine Corps Staff Sergeant Kenneth Phillips, was describing the siege of Khe Sanh by North Vietnamese Army Regulars. He was at Khe Sanh until last August and after only three months back in the States; he was here for a second tour. I didn't ask, because Khe Sanh was heavy on his mind.

Ken was saying, "Yeah. That's TV news, alright. My wife had the same idea as you until I explained that Khe Sanh Combat Base was not on a mountaintop. Actually, it was on relatively flat ground–a plateau. It even had an airstrip."

"But, what about the photos showing the rugged rocky top of a mountain where there was definitely no place to build an airstrip?"

"Those were really several hilltops in the photos and footage you saw, not just one. That's where we setup listening posts on high ground. We wanted the high ground so we could defend KSCB. Funny thing about the high ground, everybody wants it–you and your enemy. If NVA troops held the hills above KSCB, as bad as things were with them farther away, it would've quickly turned into a turkey shoot. It would've been over real quick–not taken months."

Puzzled and still remembering TV news footage from when I was in Texas, I found myself frowning and nodding. "So, what about our patrols that I heard were surrounded by NVA troops?"

"Patrols went out regularly to probe the NVA positions. What made the news is when one got into trouble. No offense, sir. But, Captain, what I've got to say ain't nothing against officers."

I shook my head. "No offense will be taken. Go ahead. Talk plain."

"Well, here's a real example. There was this green-ass second lieutenant who took his platoon out on patrol and spotted three NVA soldiers. The NVA guys ran. The lieutenant ordered his men to join him in an attempt to capture the three men. These fellas were decoys and led that platoon straight into a perfect ambush. The NVA company commander had correctly anticipated the route our patrol would take."

"Hmm. Eh, how'd the enemy commander do that?"

"No magic. This is elementary infantry stuff that both sides know. It's all about reading the terrain and asking yourself, if I'm the bad guy looking to kill me, what're his options given this landscape?"

"Oh."

"You can guess the end of the story. Yes, only a handful of men from that platoon made it back to their hilltop stronghold. And if they were wounded, *and* they made it back, there was low probability of being medevac'd out."

"So, that was because the enemy had the hills surrounded?"

"Yes. That and the weather.

"But let me be sure you understand. The entire KSCB was surrounded, not just our hilltops. During the battle for KSCB, about five thousand of us lived in mud, returned fire, and slept in the rain. The monsoon was on. It rained every day. On a good day, the clouds would lift by midday so we could get 'copters and 130's in to drop stuff on the airstrip–not land and offload. But the hilltops were shrouded most of the time."

Ken tapped the table with his forefinger. "Now, add this to the picture. We were under rocket and artillery fire day and night–but especially intense fire when aircraft showed up."

"What happened to the wounded?"

Ken shrugged. "Some bled out."

"Damn."

More drinks arrived. We were silent for a time, each man alone with his memories and demons. Here was another marine who did his job no matter the enemy's shelling or the weather. Why was I not already back doing my job?

Still turning my drink glass in its water track on my coaster, I broke the silence. "Say, Ken, did your guys get most of the supplies we dropped at KSCB?"

"Oh, that reminds me to thank you. You Air Force guys really know your shit when it comes to air delivery–whether bombs or supplies. To answer your question, we got most of it–nearly all the Air Force dropped. Marines can fly 130s, but they aren't nearly as good at putting supplies where we could get'em as your guys are."

"Thanks. I'll pass it on. News footage didn't say whose C-130s dropped stuff that the VC got.

"What'd the Air Force do different?"

"Your guys adapted to the situation and instead of landing to off-load, they flew over the airstrip and did a 'touch-and-go'. Between the 'touch' and the 'go,' moving at a bit more than one hundred miles per hour, they deployed an extraction 'chute that pulled a cargo pallet out the rear of the airplane. That took brains and balls! With great skill, they did all this under intense fire. The first time we saw this done, all the ground-pounding marines like me cheered and applauded."

"Wow!"

"Lemme take you back to the thought I was turning over in my head when you showed up. The thing that galls the hell outta me is I no longer understand what the hell we're fighting for."

"Well, don't look at me. I don't know, either. Understanding our purpose here is well above my pay grade."

"Going on nine years now, I've been a marine–an infantryman. That's all I know. That's what I do–and, even if I say so myself, I'm damn good at it. But, that's all over now. The bastards have worn me down. I'm done. Soons I reach Pendleton, I'm fuckin' out."

Turning in my chair to look squarely into Ken's face, I said, "Are you ready to give up your investment of time and energy in the Corps?"

"While I was home for those three months, I thought about it a lot. Yes, I've decided. There's a big-ass construction project starting this year to build a huge new airport for my hometown, Dallas, and Fort Worth. I'll try my hand at construction."

"Was it Khe Sanh?"

"In part, it was. The thing is, I noticed stuff I couldn't have imaged in the old days–like squabbles between generals that hit the press. Generals fought over whether we should even be at KSCB or not, and then who should own the planes that supported KSCB and worse. The first of two worse things was giving up KSCB after we had soaked the ground with American blood. You know, just like that." Ken snapped his fingers. "We just packed up and left. The second was when the NVA, using tanks, artillery, and infantry, overran the Army Special Forces compound at nearby Lang Vei. A chicken-shit marine regimental commander refused to send a relief mission to bring the survivors to KSCB. I couldn't believe it. A *marine* refusing to rescue fellow Americans... This ain't the Corps my dad joined in World War II. What the hell ever happened to 'leave no man behind'?"

Ken's long face was back. He was quiet again. No appropriate words came to my mind, so I said nothing. I was hesitant, but I reached out and patted his forearm. It felt odd to comfort a white man–especially to touch him.

I stood to leave. We shook hands and I said, "Good luck in Dallas. Semper Fi."

The marine blinked back tears.

* * *

Shortly after my return to Danang, my CO called me. When I arrived in his office, he greeted me with a big grin, leaned back in his chair, and said, "Carl, did I hear you say some time back that you have a friend in Bangkok?"

Puzzled and frowning, I answered, "Yes, sir. Did something happen to him?"

"No, no. Hold on." He fished a paper from a stack on his desk and shoved it toward me. "Take this and why don't you go on over there and see how he's faring."

The paper was authorization for my second out-of-country R&R–an unusual thing. This time it was to Bangkok, Thailand.

It was my turn to grin. "Yes, sir! I'll consider that an order!"

* * *

My friend, Bob, met me at the Bangkok Airport. That was his first act of kindness as a gracious host. At his home, a bungalow where several walls were glass, he introduced me to his household–first to his sweetheart or 'telock,' then his maid, and finally, his interpreter–three women! An old guy expression that I thought I understood suddenly became very clear with new meaning: "Don't take me to the Promised Land; take me to Thailand!"

In his home and about the city, Bob wined and dined me. He was a great host. Bob, an AT&T engineer whom I had met on one of his occasional trips to Danang, shared his munificent living with me–something residing in Rocket City can soon make one forget. I thought, *While I'm here, I'll enjoy and remember every moment.*

Too soon, it was time to return to Danang. My three days in Bangkok were like a slow curveball–a hitter's delight. The relaxed time and leisurely pace of life made me a wee bit envious of Bob. While I wished him well, Bob's life was the opposite of the tensions I sensed in Danang where actual attacks and the constant threat of rocket attacks felt like head-high fastballs–coming in tight.

On our way to the airport, I remembered a conversation with Alex during our R&R in Sydney, Australia. At breakfast on our next to last day in Sydney, Alex and I agreed that the warm welcome we received from Australian women was one more reason for the stories we'd heard about G.I.s deserting and remaining in Australia. The combination of willing women, the absence of rocket fire, and lack of anti-African-Americanism in Sydney was tempting. Though we debated the matter for a while, in our heart of hearts, we knew we would return to Danang on time and complete our tours of duty with dignity. Bangkok was even more tempting than Sydney. I didn't say so, but in Sydney, as now in Bangkok, Mama's voice spoke inside my head, "Son, remember, your word is your bond."

* * *

Later the same week, I was alone again in the chapel for prayer. On my mind was the plight of the marine corporal whose name I couldn't remember, Bill Cobb's often avowed determination to live, Chaplain Bates' counsel, Ken's imminent departure from the Marine Corps, and the possibility of flying Boeing 707s. So was Mama.

Chaplain Bates revived my memory of a forgotten conversation between Uncle George and Mr. Jimmy about shell-shock and battle fatigue. So, Ted Williams flew again the next day and in due time, resumed his Hall of Fame baseball career. Chaplain Bates told me later that his football coach's habit was on the next play after a fumble, give the ball to the guy who fumbled.

Perhaps, there's a simple lesson here for me. The longer I wait to fly combat missions, the more difficult it will be. That was already the case and it would only get worse as time passed. I want flying in my future, but I don't have to always fly for the Air Force. For now, I will do my duty. Sitting in the chapel, I resolved several matters and set a new heading for myself.

I realized that the officer's club and Jack Daniels were not helping me. When I had my fill of Jack, strangely, I felt sorry for myself. How could that be? With God's help, I had landed a burning airplane and saved the lives aboard. So, I decided to keep Jack away from my tangled web.

Next, I promised myself I'd spend regular time in the chapel, just like I did back home at Little Shiloh Baptist Church. Further, because I was so thankful to God for my life and now realized that no day is guaranteed to anyone, I committed that I would tell Mama and my siblings that I love them in every letter. I even did my best to give up hating my enemies.

I knew Mama would agree with my new heading. So would my hometown pastor, Reverend Betts. I had made a commitment to the Air Force. *I will keep my word; I will do my duty.* Forthwith, I will resume flying combat missions. Yes, I'm sure Mama would approve–actually, she would insist that I keep my word.

* * *

A few days later, I was in the crew room listening to the familiar preflight briefing as I prepared for my first combat mission since the burning airplane. The previous evening, my nightmare returned vivid and terrifying. But I had found a place of solace to help steel my splintered nerves. I recited a simple prayer; over and over. *"God, please help me remember I have nothing to fear for, you are with me."* I would not be deterred by a dream. When morning broke, I focused on my love of flying and a repeat of Mama's words to get me to the crew room.

Seated beside me was a senior pilot, an aviator in whose skills I had supreme confidence. My squadron commander had agreed to pair me with an experienced pilot who could take control if the need arose. To my surprise, all the squadron's pilots and support personnel were there to wish me well and see me off.

My nerves reminded me of the hour before my first solo flight–a mild case of butterflies. There was a great difference in how I felt climbing into the cockpit for my first sortie in a while over enemy territory, compared to shuttling a C-47 from the coast of Vietnam to Taipei by way of Hong Kong. It was then that my case of butterflies went from mild to severe, for my video of the burning plane hit the start button– again. In anticipation of enemy ground fire, that blasted tape sent my angst from high to higher. Thankfully, by the time we were halfway through the preflight checklist; I had calmed down and was feeling at home again in the cockpit.

Taxiing the C-47 toward runway 17R for my first post-disaster combat mission and hearing the staccato rhythm of her engines, I found myself nodding my head. I had just confirmed for myself that flying would indeed remain my life's work. There was a familiar tingle of anticipation in my spine when in my headphones I heard the tower say: "Paper Tiger Two-One, you're cleared for takeoff on one-seven Romeo."

Chapter 4:
Living in Rocket City

Whump! Whump!

The sound of two 120mm rockets exploding between my dorm and the east runway woke me at 0235, Monday, March 24. Then I heard the wavering sound of the Red Alert siren. At their favorite time of night, the Viet Cong were treating Danang Air Base to another fireworks display. Damn them!

"Carl!"

Still struggling to get my boots on, I yelled back to Bill, "I'm up! I'm coming! I'm coming!"

Whump!

Bill yelled, "Man, get yo' ass movin'!"

Out of breath, Dick rushed into my room and inspected me in a glance. "Damn, Carl. Bill, never mind. I've got'im!"

With one hand, Dick latched onto my arm. I felt myself being propelled into the hallway. Outside of our dormitory, with boot strings flapping, I ran to keep up with Dick, who like Bill, was taller than I. I heard boots to my right. MJ had caught up with us. We were a hodge-podge of special ops pilots–odd birds flying strange birds. We were a motley thrown-together group and very unlike my Tennessee State and officer club African American friends, who flew the newest F-4 Phantoms, sleek jet fighter-bombers. Most of my friends, the elite F-4 jocks, lived in a different dormitory.

In my dorm, we were as diverse as the aircraft we flew–alike in only one way–slow, very slow. Dick Dumas was a Louisiana mulatto and navigator on C-123s that flew low and slow spraying Agent Orange on Vietnam's lush green foliage. Mario Juliano, also known as MJ, and Bill Walsh were from New York's Little Italy and Boston, respectively. Bill and MJ flew the new small two seater observation planes we called the 'Oscar Deuce,' though the Air Force called it the O-2. The ugly little airplane had two engines, one mounted on the nose and the other aft, behind the cabin. Like a strange science-fiction insect, the thing actually had two vertical stabilizers. To support our propaganda mission, Bill and MJ's Oscar Deuces had been modified with a large loud speaker installed under the right wing. A special leaflet or 'bullshit dispenser' was installed in the floor. Effectiveness meant Bill and MJ also flew low and slow, which drew enemy fire. They depended on their steel seats for protection from enemy small arms fire. Dick and his C-123 crew mates retrofitted their ancient aircraft and sat on steel plates.

Whump! Whump!

Between the sounds of rockets exploding, I heard many boots running. Bill arrived at the bunker first and stopped. Others were stopping behind us, and like us, they were hitting the ground and lying flat.

A voice from the rear of our queue that I didn't recognize said, "Move it up there! Get the fuck in the bunker! Quick!"

Whump!

Ignoring the voice, Bill said, "Did anybody bring a flashlight?"

Dick was crawling past Bill when he said, "I've got one."

The red beam from Dick's World War II army-style flashlight barely illuminated parts of the interior of the dank moldy smelling bunker. The bunker was an in-ground pit with a roof covered by three layers of sandbags.

Whump!

From the rear, came the new guy's voice again, agitated this time. "Dammit, let's get the hell inside!"

Then MJ said over his shoulder, "Hey, newbie. Shut the fuck up! Tell you what, bring yo' scrawny ass up here and be first in with the snakes."

The newbie's attitude changed. And his voice went down ten decibels. "Oh-h. O-okay, ya'll take yo' time."

Whump!

Dick scanned and handed me the flashlight. "Here, take a look. See if I missed anything. No snakes could mean big-ass rats aplenty."

I made a quick scan. "All I see are spider webs."

In the darkness, I could *hear* the grin on Dick's face when he said, "Well, you've got the light and you're blocking the doorway. So go on in."

"Touché."

Whump!

I didn't want to be first in, but I went. So I slid in and maneuvered myself into position with my back against the front wall beside the entrance forcing others to choose; go farther into the bunker or remain outside and risk being hit by red hot pieces of enemy shrapnel.

After the last man had made his way inside, a rocket exploded nearby. Whump!

My ears were ringing from the near miss - yet I heard MJ speak. Though he was only three feet from me, he sounded far away. "Well, newbie, the VC just welcomed yo' ugly ass to 'Rocket City.'"

A chorus of gallows laughter filled the bunker. Our hilarity was not the belly laughs heard in the Officer's Club. My comrades had one thought in mind–surviving another rocket attack. Then we were quiet for a time, each man reflecting on what was dear.

* * *

As dawn broke over Danang, aka 'Rocket City,' I gave thanks for another day. In keeping with my new committed heading of doing all I could do to get home safely, I washed down my first malaria pill since arriving in Vietnam with water cupped in my palm from a dorm faucet. I thought, *If the pills hadn't hurt Bill Cobb, they won't hurt me*. Actually, I never believed the ridiculous rumor going around Danang Air Base that African Americans couldn't get malaria. I thought, *Hmmm, Africans get malaria.* I wondered;

did the rumor start as part of a conspiracy to convince African Americans not to guard against malaria?

* * *

With a mug full of mess hall decaf in hand at breakfast, I asked, "Did we lose any people or planes last night?"

Dick reported, "'*Good Morning, Vietnam*' said we didn't lose any planes, and none were even damaged."

"It seems as though a lotta rockets were fired not to hit a single plane."

Chewing bacon, Bill said, "You know what, those VC rockets ain't guided missiles. A marine told me the VC set rockets up for firing propped at some angle based on dead reckoning and use timers to set'em off in the middle o' our sleep."

I laughed. "Yeah, anytime between midnight and 0330." Then I frowned. "That doesn't explain how cum the VC more and more are missing their targets; which, by the way, is fine with me. But what's a surprise is hearing the rockets aren't fired by real people."

MJ set his coffee mug on his tray. Leaning back with a satisfied grin he said, "Well, Carl, my friend, that's because me and ol' Bill in our brand spanking new Oscar Deuces brought pee-inducing fear from the sky on the VC."

Bill laughed loud and long, slapping the table.

Dick and I exchanged glances. Holding out my hand with the palm up, I said, "MJ, what the fuck *are* you talking about? Are you spiking your coffee again?"

Now Dick joined. "I get it. You dropped a shit load o' leaflets on their heads makin' em hurry and screwed up their aim."

MJ looked amused and leaned back further. "You got part of it right. Yeah, the haste part is correct." Bill was still laughing. MJ's satisfied grin broadened. "Instead o' rainin' bullshit, we spot'em settin' up and call in the coordinates of the clearings where they are. The ops boys then light up VC asses with artillery and air strikes."

Dick stopped laughing.

I said, "Wow! No shit?"

"No shit!"

Rubbing my head, I said, "Oh, man, I had no idea. Forgive me for calling yo' little ugly-ass airplane ugly." Joining the laughter, I said, "From nigh on, I ain't calling anything ugly that can make the VC miss."

Dick said, "Yeah, we gonna show respect for y'all and your lil' funny-looking cartoon airplane."

With a sigh and an unusual dour face, Bill said, "Back to damage, guys. The word is that one Air Force guy was WIA. But, lemme tell ya, those damn rockets did kill a bunch o' people."

"Huh?"

Bill turned to me and said, "I heard a couple o' mama-sans this morning tell an AP that several rockets overshot the base and hit houses just outside of our eastern perimeter. According to them, two to three blocks into the city, whole Vietnamese families were wiped out in their sleep."

That people died in their sleep reminded me of a fellow pilot in my psyops unit who died in his sleep when his dormitory in Pleiku was hit by rocket fire in a few weeks ago. I thought, *Damn.*

Oscar Deuces or, no that shit could still happen at Danang. Well, Bob's safe in Bangkok, though Thailand didn't help Rex....

I shook my head and repeated aloud, "Damn." A few seconds later, I added, "This fuckin' war can't be over soon enough."

Part Two: Reflections

Chapter 5:
"If you want, you can fly."

On another typical day at Danang after flying two combat sorties and having dinner with the boys at the officer's club, I returned to my dorm room and wrote a letter to Mama. Before I signed it, I found I was staring at the wall beyond my small desk. My mind had drifted back to Madison....

Transported back in time, I looked beyond the wall in front of me into a clear Alabama sky. I saw Mama and Bobbie. Mama was elbow-deep in wash water and suds on a spring Monday. She was quiet and moved a white shirt of mine up and down with an easy rhythm against her ruffled ancient scrub board set in a #10 washtub. Bobbie was carrying a wicker basket of wet clothes to hang; leaving her station at a second #10 tub used for rinse. Both tubs were mounted on the same set of two-by-six's perched on saw-horses. My job was keeping the fire hot under the iron wash pot set on three concrete blocks about ten feet away. I also had the back breaking task of fetching water from the well to maintain a steady supply of hot water for Mama and Bobbie.

Boom!

The Earth shook. It sounded like a dynamite explosion. Though we were in the backyard, I could hear the panes rattle in the kitchen window. If we had been inside, as always, we would have heard picture frames vibrate against the walls and the dishes tinkle. In a loud voice, I yelled, "Ma, there goes another one!"

"Quiet, boy! The noise from that 'jit' is enough!"

Many decibels lower, I mumbled, "Oh, sorry. I forgot."

Bobbie was snickering, then made a face and stuck out her tongue. I did my best to ignore her. What I had forgotten was to keep my mouth shut for the fifteen minutes that "America's mother of the air, the 'Ma Perkins'" radio soap opera was broadcast. Mama had set the radio on a chair in the kitchen doorway long before time for her favorite daytime daily serial. Mama worked briskly while listening to every word of her beloved soap. Speaking of which, Mama had a box of her trusty Oxydol detergent beside her tub. By now, in 1955, she no longer used her homemade soap. And, of course, Oxydol sponsored "Ma Perkins."

Another jet airplane had passed over Madison causing a sonic boom. As usual, I didn't see this one either. On rare occasions, I would glimpse a streaking silver jet airplane with a blunt nose and wings that joined the fuselage at ninety degree angles. (I couldn't see the open air-intake in the nose.) I reminded myself that I needed to catch my older friend, Joe Haynes, on the next weekend and ask him again for all he could learn about the jet airplanes that passed over Madison. Mama had told me that if anybody in town could find out, it would be Joe. Joe was a professional hire at the Army's Redstone Arsenal close to Huntsville.

After we spotted the first jet airplane several years before, Mama and I had talked many times about how much I wanted to be a pilot. Bobbie was skeptical, but Mama encouraged me.

Mama interrupted my reverie, "Okay, 'Ma Perkins' has finished for today. Bring me another bucket o' hot water and tell me what all that yellin' was 'bout."

* * *

In the evening, after the "Lone Ranger and Tonto" had ridden into the radio sunset, Mama called me to where she sat in her favorite chair by a floor-standing lamp. She had her Bible on her lap. I sat on the floor and she put her hand on my shoulder and said, "Son, I'm mindful that you so much wanna be a pilot. I've told you many times since we saw the first 'jit' plane, if you believe you can and commit yourself, you can become a pilot. Do you believe in yourself?"

I nodded and said, "Yessum."

"Now, listen to these words from the Lawd: *But those who hope in the Lord will renew their strength. They will <u>soar on wings</u> like eagles; they will run and not grow weary, they will walk and not faint.*"

In unison, Bobbie and I said, "Wow!"

Sitting in a trance-like state and letting the words wash over my mind again and again, I was momentarily speechless. I was especially enamored of the part that said, *"soar on wings like eagles."*

Mama smiled. "Carl, if you want, you can fly. Believe in yourself and trust in the Lawd."

"Yessum. I will. Mama, where did you find that verse?"

"I read from Isaiah chapter 40, verse 31."

* * *

"Did you know the speed of sound was seven hundred sixty-one miles-per-hour at sea level? Well, they have a new jet plane coming out next year that can fly faster than sound at sea level!" I had finally caught Joe Haynes at home on a Saturday morning. Though some time had passed since I asked him to learn all he could about the jet airplanes, he was still excited to share the electrifying details he had learned.

"No. I learned about the speed of light in science class, but nothing about sound."

"Well anyway, the jets we hear over Madison are most likely the F-84 Thunderjets. They belong to the 31st Fighter Wing stationed over there at Turner Air Force Base next to Albany, Georgia.

"Wow! Thunderjets! That's the right name for'em, alright!" Wild-eyed, I asked, "How fast can they go?"

"Hotdog, you ain't gonna believe this, but an ex-Air Force guy told me the F-84 can do six hundred twenty-two miles-per-hour when the pilot holds the petal to the metal."

Disappointed, I said, "Aw, that's not faster than sound. You told me it has to punch through the sound barrier to make that boom."

"Yeah, but I forgot to tell you that altitude and temperature affect the speed of sound. So, in a certain temperature range at 36,000 feet, the speed of sound is only six hundred sixty-one miles-per-hour."

Puzzled, I frowned. "What does that mean?"

"Oh, the F-84 can climb to a smidgen more than 40,000 feet."

"So?"

"Well, in a dive from way up there, it seems possible an F-84 could be faster than sound for a few seconds."

Grinning like I'd hit a home run, I said, "Wow! Not bad. I can't wait until it's my turn to go faster than sound!"

"By the way, that may be dangerous for an F-84."

"How cum?"

"According to my F-84 source, he thinks the damned thing might get damaged because it wasn't designed for supersonic flight."

With concern creasing my forehead, I asked, "What's supersonic?"

"Faster than sound." Joe tilted his head and looked down into my eyes and said, "Chin up, my little friend. You're just twelve years old. By the time you're old enough, the Air Force will have something way faster than the new supersonic F-100s that the 31st is gettin' next year."

The thought was thrilling. I felt my face grin.

Joe said, "That's the way. You're grinning like the Brooklyn Dodgers have already won the pennant. By the way, how're they doing?"

I shoved both fists into the air. "Go Bums! The Dodgers lead the second-place Cubs by ten and a half games!"

* * *

Things change.

By 1958, I had graduated from junior high and was poised for the long daily bus ride to Council Training High School, the high school for colored in the county. Mama had married Mr. Archie Langford. Jackie Robinson had retired. The Dodgers had moved to Los Angeles and the 31st Fighter Wing had flown off to Germany in their sleek swept-winged F-100s.

The change in me was an even greater desire to fly. And, also very important to me, I "retired" from picking cotton!

* * *

"Hey, Carl, com'on back heah and let's see whatcha got fer us today." That was one of the seniors at Council Training High School seated on the last row of the school bus. Grinning, I thought, *This oughta be a good sales day*. Virgil and I had just boarded the bus. My guy in the back of the bus was a senior and co-captain of the football team. Since I was only a sophomore, it helped to have an upperclassman as a booster of my small enterprise.

Arriving at the back of the bus, three guys approached. One asked a question I had often heard. In a solicitous falsetto sing-song voice, he asked, "Hey, brother man, this time, can I git five for a dime and a nickel?"

"Why, hell no!"

Shaking a finger at my face and in a belligerent voice, he said, "Uh-huh. You jes wait 'n' see if me 'n' my boys hep you 'n' Virgil out next time y'all gittin' yo' asses kicked down there at the Bottom."

"Keep yo' hep. You know the drill. Pay up. Hand over a dime and you git three. Or, if you gonna be cheap today, gimme a nickel for one."

The guy frowned. "Why you lil' sawed-off mutha, you tryin' be a hard-ass."

The co-captain said, "Calm down, man. Stop actin' dumb. You already know Carl's prices. So shut the fuck up and pay the man."

And so it went. While Virgil stood watch for the principal, sales at school in the boy's toilet were brisk. I sold twenty cigarettes or a whole pack, one or three at a time, before classes began. The weight of the coins distributed in two pockets felt good. By the end of lunch period, I had sold the second pack of the usual two I brought to school each day. At the end of the school-day, I counted gross sales at one dollar sixty cents, less cost of goods sold at twenty-five cents a pack, or fifty cents, for a net profit of one dollar ten cents. The day turned out to be another typical business day for my thriving little enterprise.

* * *

$1 in 1958 was worth $8.27 in 2015 dollars.

* * *

I learned my sales tactics from Mr. Archie Langford, my stepdad. He owned the grocery store where I worked when I was not in school. Though the store was my supplier of cigarettes, I bought at retail from Mr. Archie–not wholesale.

In 1958, the colored community of Madison was still centered on Pension Row and the streets it connected. Colored commerce, churches, schools, and providers of professional services, such as teachers, barbers, beauticians, and others were all on or close to "the Row." Mr. Archie's grocery store sat near the geographic center of the community. His successful business thrust Mr. Archie into the realm of influential people about Madison. My life changed and took on a heading not possible before Mama married Mr. Archie.

Instead of laboring in the cotton fields that fall, my new job was opening the store each morning before six o'clock. As fall turned to winter, I made the short trek to the store in the dark, past cars and plants coated with frost. My first task in the store was to start a coal fire in the potbelly stove, open for business, and return home in time to dress and board the school bus at half past six. The pockets of coloreds scattered about large rural Madison County meant the misfortune of a long circuitous bus ride to our only high school–located down the hill and across a highway from the Alabama Agricultural and Mechanical College, a segregated institution for coloreds.

Besides general merchandise, we sold and delivered coal. Our coal was priced at sixteen dollars per ton, or when purchased in smaller quantities, one dollar per hundred pounds–the equivalent of a #10 washtub filled with coal. Loading and delivering coal from our coal yard reminded me of Tennessee Ernie

Ford's 1955 number-one hit song, "Sixteen Tons." Unlike the song, I didn't end by owing my soul to the company store. Instead, my reward for working in the store was earnings from Mr. Archie.

Mr. Archie's discount pricing for a larger quantity of coal led me to use the same logic in pricing the cigarettes I sold.

* * *

"Man, you're gonna throw us late again. You know Joe don't like to wait on nobody, including yo' narrow...." Virgil, standing in the doorway of our front room, was expressing exasperation with my tardiness.

I cut Virgil off before he could let slip the word "ass" in earshot of Mama in the next room. "Yeah, yeah, I know Joe Haynes doesn't like waiting. Just hold yo' hoss 'til I wash this coal dust off."

In 1960, the year that Kennedy was elected, we were seniors at Council Training. On that chilly November Saturday night we planned to ride out to the Bottom with our older bachelor friend, Joe Haynes. By my calculation, we would arrive at the Bottom in plenty of time for the regular Saturday night social– Wurlitzer music, girls, dancing, and fried fish on "loaf bread samiches." Oh, and watch the fights among those gathered. Of course, I had never mentioned the fights to Mama.

Before I took two steps, Bobbie passed through the room and said, "Save time. Don't waste a minute on that face o' your'n. Fixin' that mangy mug will take more time than y'all have. Besides, Lucy Mae

Struthers won't care; if she kin git you to spend yo' lil' money on her."

Shaking my head, I laughed in spite of myself. I heard Mama try to stifle a laugh. Virgil laughed so hard that he leaned against the door frame to remain afoot. By the time I thought of a rejoinder, it was too late. Bobbie was already out the door and on the porch.

Dressed and ready for the evening, I could hear Joe and Virgil talking in the front room. Mama summoned me into her room. She stopped sewing and gazed into my eyes. With growing unease, I stood waiting for her to speak. I was wearing my expensive store-bought duds and the highest priced shoes found in Madison-Huntersville. With the money I made and the clothes I wore, I was given the choice of girls who lined up to date me.

Mama motioned me closer. "Son, I want you to remember, clothes do not make the man."

Trying to figure out what I could safely say, my forehead felt warm. At length, I said, "Though Mr. Archie, ain't my dad, I'm jes to tryin' dress like him."

Mama's face took on a new stern expression. She pointed at my face and just above a whisper, said, "Boy, you listen to me and you listen good. First, Archie Langford is the *only* dad you got. Don't you *ever* forget it. Second, people in Madison, colored and white, respect him because he's a fine upstanding man, not because o' what he puts on his back."

Chastened and about to break into a sweat, I could think of nothing to say but, "Yessum."

"I'ma let you go now. But you remember this lil' talk and what yo' grams said. 'A third-class somebody is always better'n a first-class nobody.'"

* * *

"Hey, Carl. Man, are you still up? The boys are waitin' in Fig's room for us to take their money." Alex was on the prowl looking for people to drag into a late-night card game.

Startled out of my memories of 1960s high school-days and back into the reality of Danang's 1969, I blinked and dropped my pen. I thought, *How long have I been staring at this wall?* Aloud, I said, "Count me out tonight. You go ahead and y'all have fun."

Chapter 6:
"Here to yonder" – Langston Hughes

Shaking his head, Fig said, "Man, oh man, if we had zigged instead o' zagging, we would've flown nose-first into that damn SAM!"

Incredulously, I asked, "If the SAM was locked onto you, how'd you escape?"

"We zagged right, and then made a pucker-tightening dive to a hundred feet above the trees. We were nearly on the damned deck! We followed that with a sharp ninety-degree left turn." Fig took a deep breath, eyes unfocused, reliving his and his front-seater's desperate dive for life. Blinking, he added, "Thank God, we shook the sombitch."

"Yes, thank God."

Using my experience flying the supersonic T-38, I visualized Fig's anxious attempt to escape the SAM (surface-to-air missile). A shudder ran the length of my spine and I involuntarily hunched my shoulders, sloshing my Jack Daniels. I tried–but only for half a second–to imagine losing Fig, my South Carolina friend and comrade from our years together in Air Force ROTC at Tennessee State University. Now living the coincidence of being assigned together, we, with Denver and other Tennessee State alumni, were deepening our friendship at Danang Air Base. I shoved a long-handled two-pronged fork firmly into my steak on the grill and flipped it. That relieved some tension in my neck and back. From the corner of my eye, I saw Denver apply the same violence to his steak. I imagined Denver was feeling the same eerie feeling of imagined loss that ran through my mind and body–yea, even my spirit.

With his eyes closed, Denver took a slow sip from his drink. Then his typical grin returned. He said, "Fig, here's what's still ringing in my ears, 'shoulda, zigged, woulda, zagged, damn sam'. So, what're you now, some frigging poet?"

Fig and I erupted into laughter. Later, I didn't remember the joke as funny. But, Denver, as was his habit, had steered us away from remorse to mirth–headed toward our usual gallows humor.

We were a trio of early arrivals at the Officer's Club for dinner. The reddest and juiciest steaks were ours without contest from the customary crowd. Hot fries straight out of the fat and our salads surrounded the finest steaks to arrive at Port Danang. Denver continued to distract Fig and me from the topic of the sophisticated Soviet Union-built radar-guided surface-to-air missiles used by North Vietnam against our elite F-4 crews. As Denver covered his steak with Worcestershire sauce, he said, "Man, when are y'all gonna grow up and become internationalists? Step outside o' that American A.1. Steak Sauce. Here, try the real deal for steaks."

Laughing, I said, "American or not, I remember you thought A.1. Sauce was great at Tennessee State when you covered your dining hall meatloaf with it!"

Before I stopped laughing at my barb, Fig declared with an impish grin, "I beg your pardon, sir. That stuff you called 'meatloaf' was the original 'wonder meat.'"

More raucous laughter.

Denver almost lost a bite of his steak. "To eat that damn 'wonder meat,' I had to smoother it with something."

With at least a spoon of sarcasm, Fig said, "Sorry, Den, but I must blow away your thought that you're leaving your alumni buddies with a domestic brand. Sir, I regret to inform you that A.1. sauce is just as British as Worcestershire sauce."

"No, shit?"

"No, shit."

"You know, hanging out with you guys is education in itself–even about steak sauce. I remember in my freshman year, we'd sometimes hang out in Carl's and Elbert's room expounding the topic of the day. I looked up to you guys because you were already sophomores."

Fig was nodding and tapping his fork against his plate. "Yeah, all learning at Tennessee State didn't happen in a classroom."

Laughing, I said, "What're you thinking–women or cards?"

Fig grinned. "It's usually women. But for a change, I had a more serious thought in mind."

Denver said, "Well, I can tell you a thing that got my attention. I loved hearing Carl and Elbert talk about how the local car dealers loved ROTC grads and retiring before age forty-five and seeing the world. That's why I signed up for the Advanced Course. I was determined to follow Carl's example of hard work toward his goal to fly."

I laughed. "Yeah, and you see where that got you–square in the middle of this crazy-ass war."

"No. Man, I'm serious. I didn't start studying until close to the end of my freshman year."

In deep thought, I was rolling a bite-size piece of steak to and fro on my plate. Presently, I said, "Denver, be careful who you follow. We damned near didn't meet. Back then, pride didn't let me admit why I had that sharp focus on my work when I was a sophomore."

"What're you telling me?"

Fig was grinning, "Den, close your face and let the man tell his story."

I began again. "Though I came to Tennessee State for the sole reason of the aviation technology program and AFROTC, I gave no thought to the possibility that one needed to do work to graduate. I had not connected hard work and dedication to getting from here to yonder. My priorities were hanging out at the Student Union, playing cards, and having a good time."

Denver stopped chewing. "You mean you ditched your dream to fly?"

"No, not directly, but in effect, I did.

"But hold up. Lemme tell ya a couple o' stories. During my sophomore year, I was desperate to hang onto my recently found discipline to do the work required to graduate and become a pilot. Then one day, inspiration that I sorely needed to solidify my resolve interrupted my lunch when it walked into the cafeteria. I stopped eating and sat with my fork standing like an antenna in my fist. I was transfixed. My eyes were glued on First Lieutenant Ed Moon's smartly tailored United States Air Force blue uniform–specifically, the wings on his chest.

"Ed had graduated from Tennessee State two years before and had also completed the Air Force's Undergraduate Pilot Training (UPT). Looking at Ed's wings added to my resolve that in spite of my poor beginning as a freshman, I would graduate and wear wings like Ed. I later learned from his younger brother that Ed was on his way to Vietnam to fly F-100s.

"Now, here's my second story. My grades in the first semester of my freshman year were so bad that I decided I'd better head-off the mail lest Mama would take out her disappointment on me."

Fig had already heard my story and was laughing. Bill Cobb joined us. He had a plate in each hand.

Denver wanted to know, "What do you mean, 'head-off the mail?'"

"The school didn't have my mama's address. I knew the registrar would mail my grades to my older sister in Chattanooga. So I raced my smart ass to Chattanooga to intercept my grades and keep'em from Mama."

Bill Cobb shook his head and sucked his teeth. "Tsk, tsk. Here's another idiot who thinks he's slick."

I ignored Bill. "My sister told me I was too late. She had already forwarded my grades to Mama. I could've saved that trip to Chattanooga."

Bill said, "Serves yo' slick-ass right. Betcha caught the hell you deserved when you got yo' ass home."

"Yep. That's exactly what happened. Mama met me at the door–and it was on!"

When the laughter stopped, neither Denver nor Fig would ask, but Bill would–and did. "Just how bad were these grades?"

"Not yet failing, but very damn close to it. Mama helped me get my butt onto a new heading for the rest of my days at Tennessee State. First, she took away half my allowance. That meant no more partying. Second, she gave me only one semester to improve my grades or that would be the end of my stay at Tennessee State–and the end of my dream to fly. Lemme tell y'all, no matter the big man I think I am my mama still has the wherewithal to change and direct my mind with a look or words. That was all the discipline I needed to return to school with dedication and the will to work hard and graduate with my commission. So, Denver, be careful who you follow."

Denver blinked several times and leaned back in his chair. Then he tugged at his chin. "It seems to me, I followed the right guy. I met you *after* your moms had lit up your ass and you were already on a corrected heading. The timing paid off for me. I owe your moms."

* * *

The boys were having before dinner suds when I busted through the door at the Officer's Club one afternoon not long before the start of monsoon. With a big grin, I yelled, "Set'em up! Gather 'round guys. I'm celebrating the big two-oh-oh tonight. Gonna party tonight!" Then, with my hands in the air and rocking side to side, I started to sing Otis Redding's hit. "Way down in Alabama, shoutin' bamalama! Way down in Louisiana...."

Bill Cobb laughed and covered his ears. "Somebody shut that fuckin' noise off while I find 'Shout Bamalama' on the jukebox for this ol' 'Bama boy."

By ten o'clock, I had lost track of how many drinks I'd had. Someone was playing "Shout Bamalama" again. The celebration of completing my two-hundredth mission was still going strong long past dinner and after several rounds of whist. Sipping my old Tennessee friend, Jackie D., I smiled at my bid whist hand. Alex and I had already won enough to pay the bar bill. Four tricks in, I could see us running a Boston on the two new players at our table, Denver and Chuck.

Denver was talking about our days at Tennessee State again. I figured his attention was divided. Denver said, "Man, I was really sorry for lil' Ben Johnson. That po' boy was forever talking about flying. You know, he was the only guy in memory to ace the Air Force Officer Qualifying Test."

Alex asked, "Wow. Do you mean to tell me, he killed that 'white folks test?'"

"Yep."

"With a performance like that, why were you sorry for him?"

"Ben had his dorm room festooned with models of the century series fighter jets. But he couldn't get into the advanced course and was dropped from the program. That broke his heart. It was like he had lost his best girl."

"Wow. Bummer. What happened?"

"He only weighed one hundred eighteen pounds."

"Oh, shit. That's a tough loss. He was close, but not close enough."

Chuck was frowning at his cards, and then glanced at me. "Yeah, real tough. You know, he was about Carl's size."

Denver laughed. "Yeah, Ben was another short, skinny, narrow-ass dude–just like Carl."

I flinched but held my tongue. I hated being called skinny or little–and worse, both.

Alex turned his whist hand face down on the table. "Wait a minute. Carl, how'd you stay in the program or even get into flight school?"

I said, "Alex, let it rest. I'm focused on taking money from these fellas. I ain't thinkin' 'bout nothing but these cards."

Denver laughed. "Alex, you're asking for two stories about how Carl got, as he would say, here from yonder."

Alex let his hand remain face down. "Well, let's hear'em."

I said, "Alex, Den's trying to distract you. That's the only way the turkey can win. Don't fall for it."

From the next table, Bill Cobb quipped, "Go ahead Den, tell Alex about the time Carl ate two pounds of bananas and puked on a medical technician."

Outnumbered, I resigned, picked up my faithful friend, Jack, and took a long swig. I held my whist hand against my chest. Grinning, I said, "Okay. Den, go ahead. Have a good laugh. We'll see who has the last laugh when we turn these cards over."

Denver waved me off. "Alex, let's do the first story first. Okay. Carl was not in as deep a hole as Ben. Carl was only two pounds underweight for his height. Ben was four pounds under. Ben didn't have a prayer."

Alex looked my way as if to size me up. "I'd say he's still underweight."

"He probably is. Anyway, an NCO friend whispered and told Carl to get somebody to weigh for him. Carl picked his friend Vandenberg to be that somebody. That weigh-in saved Carl's ass with just one pound over the minimum."

I chimed in, "The whole thing was about my life's career. So I thanked God and hugged Vandenberg."

Alex said, "Wow. Okay, what's the second story? Or was Cobb exaggerating as usual?"

Cobb said, "Watch it, turkey! I heard that. If Carl didn't puke on that tech, grits ain't grocery and Mona Lisa was a man."

Denver was laughing and stuttering, "C-C-Carl, was still underweight when he reported for pilot training. This time, no one down in South Texas could weigh for him. The medical tech on duty must've felt sorry for him. So the guy says, 'Sir, we've got a problem. Here's what you do. Go down to the commissary and buy two pounds of bananas. Eat everyone of'em. Drink water and come straight back to me.' Our boy was happy to do it; anything to save his career. After doing as he was told, the tech weighed Carl and he met the requirement."

I said, "Again, I thanked God for the tech and saving my career. That tech was another link in the chain of people getting me from here to yonder."

Now Denver was laughing so hard that he could no longer talk. So I said. "Okay, let's be done with this story so I can take s'more o' y'all's money. Okay, Alex, before I stepped on the scale, I began to feel sick. Before I could get off the scale, I upchucked everything I'd eaten that day. I tried to turn away, so did the tech. Neither of us was fast enough."

Now Alex joined in laughing with everyone within earshot. He struggled to talk. "Th-th-the d-d-dude does you a h-h-huge favor and you r-r-reward him with two pounds of damn vomit!"

* * *

One morning on the flight line while headed for my airplane, I paused at the roar from four F-4 Phantoms from Bee Settles' wing rolling to takeoff positions on runway three-five-Romeo, and then watched them launch in two-by-two formations. Their landing gear retracted nearly in unison and I was reminded of my Undergraduate Pilot Training (UPT) days at Laughlin Air Force Base, Texas. Their roar was sweet as the bomb-laden F-4s climbed at thirty degrees. Last year, it was me in my T-38 roaring down the runway in formation with another T-38. But first, before I could roar, I had to purr in the little prop Cessna T-41, and then tweet in the jet T-37.

I still have fond and proud memories of UPT....

While I was a transportation officer at Shaw Air Force Base, South Carolina, waiting for a slot in the United States Air Force Undergraduate Pilot Training School at Laughlin, I was chomping at the bit and anxious to get on with the next steps toward becoming a pilot. Arriving at Laughlin and confronted with the rigor of UPT academics and the need to develop flying skills on a rigid schedule caused some reflection and self-examination. In an instant, pilot training looked more like a rugged mountain that a hill. Even with my degree in aviation technology, the UPT syllabi and pace gave me pause.

Upon learning what was expected and understanding the failure rate for student pilots was thirty-eight percent, I had reason to wonder whether indeed UPT was more than I had bargained for. Instructors had warned us, time and again, not to fall behind in our studies because it would be impossible to catch up. Besides, student pilots needed to have read and understood the actions that were required in the cockpit before situations arose. So UPT was the last hurdle and it stood between me and the realization of my childhood dream to fly. Early, I decided there would be no time for a repeat of my first semester at Tennessee State.

From Isaiah 40:31, I read again. *"But those who hope in the Lord will renew their strength. They will soar on wings like eagles."* Then, and throughout my time in UPT, I prayed.

The first airplane my class flew was the T-41A Mescalero. The plane was an off-the-shelf copy of the popular civilian high-winged Cessna 172 Skyhawk with fixed non-retractable landing gear. The Cessna 172/T-41 was a basic light utility airplane. Our T-41 instructors were contractors hired by the Air Force for the first of three phases in pilot training.

Six weeks later, we graduated from phase one and began six months of training in the "Tweetie Bird." Though popularly known as the Tweetie Bird, the Air Force had designated this funny-looking two seat side-by-side jet training airplane as the T-37. Some said it sounded like a screech owl and had doors that resembled those of a barn. Others said it looked like a tadpole. Nonetheless, I was happy to fly T-37s, for they were my introduction to the jet age.

In the T-37 phase, Air Force instructors reminded us again, "This program will not get any easier. Don't fall behind. If you think keeping up is hard, once behind, it's damned near impossible to catch up. Get to know your tablemates today, because tomorrow one of you won't be here." As students were dropped from the program for poor academics or subpar flying skills,

I prayed again and promised myself that I will do my best classroom and field work.

During the T-37 phase, it was difficult not to notice the phase-three student pilots strutting about as if walking on clouds. They were the elites among students, for they flew the new supersonic trainer, the T-38. According to them, they were the ultimate of the pharaohs, untouched by human hands, well above us lesser mortals who flew the tiny slow funny-looking guppy-resembling humble T-37.

Ode to Joy! Of course, when I graduated from the six-month T-37 program and entered phase three and flew the T-38, I behaved just as the previous T-38 class had. Once in the T-38, one's ego did grow. We flew what some called the "White Rocket" or the "White Broomstick." The T-38 Talon and its close cousin, the formidable F-5 Freedom Fighter, were lightweight supersonic airplanes powered by twin engines whose design was based on engines previously created for missiles (rockets).

My first flight in a T-38 was one I will never forget. A student's first time in a T-38 is called the "dollar ride." Of course, during my dollar ride, my instructor, Captain Lattrell, had the controls and I sat in the backseat. Captain Lattrell rolled into takeoff position on runway three-one-Charlie, the center runway of three at Laughlin. He advanced the throttles to one-hundred percent, released the brakes, and then eased the throttles further forward to light the afterburners. From that point, things happened very fast–too fast for me. At the one-thousand-foot marker, our speed was about one-hundred-fifteen miles per hour. With our quickening pace, the one-thousand-foot markers along the runway looked to me like a picket fence. Seconds later we reached one-hundred-seventy-eight MPH and rotated for takeoff. Accelerating at an even more incredible rate, the airplane leapt from the runway. Captain Lattrell retracted the gear and flaps. Over the far end of the runway, we were passing a speed of Mach 0.9 (90% of the speed of sound). We climbed at forty-five degrees, which felt like straight up to me. Still just minutes later, Lattrell brought us level at 40,000. My mind had been left and was still in the takeoff roll! Up there, on my dollar ride, I experienced my first supersonic flight.

At a lower altitude, I learned that the T-38 can roll 720 degrees per second. I found this out in level flight when Captain Lattrell snapped the stick to the left causing the right side of the canopy to whack my helmet as we began a triple aileron roll. Wow! Our T-38 made two revolutions around the airplane's longitudinal axis in one second! That taught me to never jerk the stick in a T-38. But Lattrell was not done yet. More acrobatics added to my eye-popping, exhilarating, and thoroughly memorable first T-38 flight.

Once in the T-38 program, I discovered why T-38 pilots had such big egos. I quickly learned that to fly the T-38, you have to be good. Student pilots, and even astronauts, made mistakes in the T-38 and crashed–and, yes, they died. In the magnificent and very fast T-38, one cannot show fear and doubt. T-38 pilots must believe if anything goes wrong, they can handle it, no matter the difficulty.

There was no doubt; my memory of UPT was one I will cherish as long as I live. Even today, I still remember the words of my squadron commander, Major Eugene Gray, just days before our graduation, "I congratulate you on becoming an Air Force pilot. You have met and conquered one of the most difficult challenges in the United States military. As you know, more than one-third of your day-one classmates failed. You persevered, you finished UPT. That makes you one of the elite members of the United States Armed Services."

Graduation day may have been the proudest day of my life. I can still picture it; my name was called, and I marched to the podium and received the silver wings of an Air Force pilot and a certificate of Aeronautical Rating. My Air Force wings meant more to me than my Tennessee State degree; for I had prayed and worked hard many years and realized my dream.

I shook my head to clear my mind and end reminiscing. Looking up, I was still in my tracks on the ramp at Danang watching the second pair of F-4s roar into the sky with their heavy munitions load. Later, as I climbed aboard my C-47, I glanced up again and whispered, "Thank you, Lord."

Settling into my aircraft commander's seat and reaching for the preflight checklist, I thought, *now that I've come this far–from there to here, I'll need to find my way from here to perhaps those commercial 707s…. From here to yonder….*

Chapter 7:
Influencers

Bar none, Mama had the greatest sway in shaping and guiding my development. Mama taught me a basic way of seeing and reacting to the world. She was my first and most influential life coach.

* * *

In the shade that afternoon, the temperature was about 32° C (90° F) and the humidity made the air thick. For May, this was not a typical Danang day. A sudden gust from the southeast off the South China Sea felt refreshing. Seconds later, we were slapping and scrambling trying to grab our playing cards from the table and patio floor. Engrossed in our bid whist game, we had not noticed the approach of a dry season thunderstorm. Now the rain began pelting us as it came in sideways on the wind. While Officers Club employees hastily secured the table umbrellas, Chuck, Denver, and Fig quickly followed me, running to get inside.

In air-conditioned comfort, we spread the cards to dry on a vacant table while Chuck peeled the cellophane off a new deck. With a fresh unlit cigarette dangling from his lips, Chuck dealt. "Before we were interrupted by the storm, Carl, what did you say Professor Ryan told you?"

Laughing, I said, "Oh, yeah. I was saying, Professor Ryan looked me dead in the eye and told me, 'Young man, you can go out there and kill yourself, but don't you put a scratch on my airplane.'" I paused. There were grins and nods around the table. "I don't mind telling you that the old fear from my first flight with Professor Ryan returned and it sent a shudder down my spine."

Fig was packing his hand carefully card by card in who knows what order as he spoke, "He must have told everyone that line. He said the same thing to my class."

Denver said, "Of course, I never flew with Professor Ryan. But I heard he had something to do with the Tuskegee Airman. Did he graduate from Tuskegee?"

I said, "Den, Professor Ryan graduated from Tennessee State. Well, you know what I mean, Tennessee Agricultural and Mechanical State Normal College. His connection to Tuskegee was as a flight instructor during the big war."

"You mean, he actually taught the guys who flew in the 99th Pursuit Squadron?"

"Yep. And the 332nd Fighter Group."

"Did he go to war with them?"

"Nope. Look, Den, will you just shut up and bid?"

Fig laughed, "Den, Professor Ryan was not in the Army Air Force. They used civilian instructors at the Tuskegee Pilot Training School." Fig changed the order of two cards in his hand. "Judging from being one of his students, I can say he was one hell of an instructor. Teaching was his bit for the war effort."

I made a big sigh. "True, Professor Ryan was not a military man." I pressed the face of my cards against my flight suit. "But, let me tell you, I haven't met a military man yet who could put the fear of God in me like Professor Ryan could. He was a no-nonsense kind of guy."

Fig said, "When Professor Ryan taught, you'd best pay close attention because if you couldn't give back what he said, woe be unto yo' hind parts. If it were a matter of doing, you'd better do whatever it was exactly as he taught you."

Leaning back in my chair, I said, "That's right. Professor Ryan was okay and calm until the second time you got it wrong. Then he would be on yo' ass like stink on a skunk."

Chuck was nodding knowingly. "That's for damn sho'. He told us several times, 'You can make one mistake flying an airplane and you may get away with it. But make two or three and you're unlikely to live to tell'."

Now I remembered Professor Ryan with great appreciation. I thought about my burning airplane as I scratched my stubble. "I'm reminded of my first flight with Professor Ryan. Aloft, he made me feel lower than whale shit." I slowly shook my head. "Back on the ground, I thought, maybe I wasn't cut out to be a pilot. Maybe I picked the wrong career. Maybe I should just forget the whole friggin' thing."

Chuck said, "Damn. The same happened to me, too."

To me, Fig said, "So what changed your mind about dropping out?"

My eyes were unfocused. Then I was staring at the table. I blinked and turned to Fig. "Professor Ryan changed my mind. He seemed to know where my head was. He said, 'Son, you can do this. How? Stay focused and dedicate your mind and soul to flying and you'll get new techniques right the first time around.' That picked me up." I paused. "Even with his gruff manner, Professor Ryan believed in me and helped me believe in me. He was an important influence on me and became one more person in the chain of life helpers along my way from here to yonder."

* * *

My friend Jack was waiting for me with a cold glass on the next table. Alex handed the dice to me. Blowing on them, I shook them twice and felt a hand on my shoulder. Bee was holding out his other hand and saying, "Gimmie."

"Aw, Bee. I'm a big boy. I can handle these lil' ol' dice and my money. Last night proves that."

Still holding his hand out, Bee wiggled his fingers and said, "Yeah. Last night it was just you. Tonight, I see you and Jack are best friends again. So, com' on, gimmie."

Alex laughed. "Bee, go the hell away and let the man roll. You're interferin' with my fuckin' money makin' business."

Now, Bee laughed. "Dude, I'm sorry about reducing the return on your investment in my brother's friend, Jack." Bee squeezed my shoulder. "Com' on, Bro, grease my palm."

I sighed and laid the dice on the table. I knew, and Bee knew, that when I drank Jack Daniels, I was lousy at craps. I guess Alex knew, too. He had won enough of my money when I had Jack with me and Bee wasn't around to safeguard my cash. So I handed over most of my money to Bee for safekeeping. Then, I took a long swig of Jackie and rolled the dice.

Skip Woodard finished his dinner and walked to our craps table with a fist full of currency. "Lemme in."

Without looking at Skip, I said, "Whoa. Hold yo' hoss, fella." I rolled again.

Skip asked, "What were you guys saying a few minutes ago about us in commercial aviation?"

Alex said, "Oh, we were just saying that it was a crime and a shame that Professor Ryan and none of the Tuskegee Airmen were hired by commercial airlines after the war."

Skip sighed. "Yeah." He took another deep breath. "What excuses did the airlines give?"

Alex continued. "Any excuse will do. How 'bout lack of multiengine experience? Or, oh, yes, how 'bout when they were in our corner and saving us from flying into a city where we may not be able to get a hotel room."

In my best sarcastic voice and with a straight face, I said, "Why, Alex, what's wrong with you, boy! You oughta show som' gratitude when these nice white people put themselves out and go to all the trouble of refusin' to hire you. It's only so's they can protect you from getting' yo'self into trouble with one o' them ol' segregated hotels." Shaking my head, I continued, "Lawd, Lawd, I just don't know where I went wrong tryin' school you. Boy, I thought I had raised you better."

When the laughter died, Skip said, "Like the rest of us, I was raised to know my place. But the thought has occurred to me more'n once that it might be a great life to fly 707s for an international airline."

Skip had the confidence to confess his dream to us; the audacity to lay out his innermost thoughts–unusual among the boys. *Involuntarily*, I glanced over my shoulder to see whether a white officer was in earshot. Immediately, I chastised myself with a harsh string of expletives inside my head for succumbing to the fear of violating the rules white Alabama, yea white American, society had planted deep in the minds of my ancestors and was passed to me by my mother because she wanted me to live. I could hear Mama in my head, "Boy, you mind the signs that say, 'Colored.' Stay in yo' place; don't you go makin' no trouble."

Though I saw Chuck make the same glance, I said nothing when our eyes locked for the briefest moment. We knew each the other's shame for yielding to the impulse to check for a white man nearby then immediately hated ourselves for guilt we were desperately trying to suppress; actually kill, remove from our souls less it stifle us. The quick eye interaction where one of us caught the other in the misdeed of a heretofore secret and hated thought brought on more shame for Chuck and me. Nothing needed to be said; we understood our mutual humiliation. We were in Vietnam but had not escaped American culture–dammit.

I shook my head to clear my mind. The 707s that I saw in Hong Kong flashed into memory. I decided it was a preposterous dream; *what was I thinking?*

Rubbing his chin, Alex leaned against the craps table. "Skip, your dream may be in reach by the time we get out."

"Yeah, times are changing. Only thirteen months have passed since Dr. King was murdered. But his legacy will continue opening doors beyond the new laws."

Chuck said, "I don't see how the Civil Rights Act of '64 is going to help you set your black buns in the cockpit of a 707."

Alex said, "I think Skip is talking about something fundamental and different from laws…."

"You mean like taking away the airlines' multiengine excuse because Skip flew eight-engine B-52s for the Air Force?"

"Let me finish. Two months after we graduated from college, the Supreme Court told Continental Airlines they could no longer refuse to hire pilots because of the color of their skin. One could argue that it happened because of the Civil Rights Act of '64. Or was it because of the Civil Rights Act of '66? Or was it because it was judged to be just plain wrong to refuse to hire a qualified applicant because of color? I think more and more, it will happen without the intervention of a court because of the latter. I think Skip and I see that as the 'King Legacy.'"

"Hold the phone! There was no Civil Rights Act of '66."

In unison, Fig and I said, "Yes, there was. 1866."

Fig continued. "There were civil rights acts in other years, including last year, but only these two are relevant here."

Denver said, "Wow. This is like back at Tennessee State. I'm still learning from you guys!"

Though I didn't say so, I was learning, too. I thought, *well, shit. Maybe the 707 dream was not so far-fetched and nutty after all.* I said, "Hey, Alex, who was that black guy that Continental hired?"

"Marlon Green."

"So he was first.... Anybody hired since Green?"

Fig said, "No. But Green was not the first black pilot hired. While Green's case was grinding its way through the courts for six damn years, American Airlines hired Dave Harris in '65. So Green was second."

* * *

At half past eleven, Thursday night, May 8, 1969, the air felt less muggy than usual. I had pushed back from the whist table and stepped out of the Officer's Club. The temperature must have been in the mid-seventies–quite pleasant. I took a deep breath of the fresh breeze coming from the southeast off the South

China Sea and stretched. Glancing up as I stretched, my attention turned to the Moon. It stood at less than a fist above the horizon. I could not recall seeing the Moon that low while showing only half its face since Madison. I tilted my head to match the line of the ten-degree diagonal slice that seemed to chop the moon's face in half.

"Boy, what the hell are you looking at? Somethin' wrong wid yo' neck?" That was Bill Cobb leaving the club behind me.

"What the hell does it look like I'm doin'? I'm gazin' at the Moon. What for? I'm trying to get my mind on something other than mistreatment from white folks."

Expecting lip as usual from Bill, my hands flew akimbo. Instead, he stood beside me looking at the Moon. He said nothing. After what must have been a whole minute, I said, "Now it's my turn. Is somethin' wrong wid yo' neck?"

"Touché." Bill folded his arms and moved his alligator skin shod feet farther apart. His plaid Ivy League cap was pulled down over his eyes just as he wore it over his sunglasses inside the club. The brown and dull-red plaid lines over a beige background of his cap were identical twins with his wide collar shirt, bellbottom trousers, and socks. Who knows where Bill found head-to-toe matching clothes in the same plaid. His tour of duty in Vietnam was nearly over and it was close to time for Bill to return to the States and leave the Air Force. And he was still, by far, the king of men's fashion at Danang Air Base–probably in all of

Vietnam. In spite of Mama's teaching that the clothes did not make the man, I felt like a ragamuffin standing next to Bill. I was clad in my usual Air Force flight suit and boots.

Above the noise of an AC-130 Spectré Gunship in its takeoff roll on runway one-seven-Lima, Bill said, "You were awfully quiet in there as the debate raged among our brothers about the path to freedom; Dr. King's way or Malcom's."

After a deep sigh, I said, "Yeah, I guess I like the paths of each."

Still looking at the Moon, Bill nodded. "I, too, don't see that either is wrong. Once upon a time, I thought 'any means necessary' was the way to go. But…." His voice trailed off.

I waited, and then asked, "But what?"

Bill looked at me. "If that means a race war where our guys are armed with only handheld weapons…." He stopped talking again. Again, I waited. This time, I said nothing.

Presently, Bill said, "Militarily, I can't see how our guys could do more than be annihilated. I'm no social scientist, but when the thing is over–that is, when the smoke from guns and bombs are gone, I don't see it *really* ending for generations."

"Huh? Generations?"

"Think about it. For generations already, whites have feared us. A war would confirm their worst fears. Nina Simone's song, 'Backlash Blues', would take on new meaning. Then, will they take on the behavior of a cornered animal?"

"Wow! I never thought of that. You must mean Langston Hughes' and Nina's line: 'Mean Old White Backlash.'"

"The same. Huh? Wait a sec. What'd you say about Langston Hughes?"

"Mr. Hughes wrote 'Backlash Blues' with Nina."

"Well, I'll be damn. I didn't know that. Little Bro, I learned something from you tonight."

"But hold on a minute. Let's get back to the debate. Didn't I hear you in there argue in favor of Stokely's method; 'burn, baby, burn'?"

"Aw, you know me. At any time, I can argue any point of view. I just did that to see where the King fellas would go. I wanted to hear where they thought the King legacy would take us or how it would help shape America's future in his absence."

"You never cease to amaze. So did you find out?"

"Yes and no. They think white folks will come to their senses and we'll all be one big happy American family."

"Do you agree?"

"Why, hell no! Too many of'em are still fighting the 'Uncivil War'. Out of their fear, they've grown to hate us to the point that they're teaching their young the same venom."

"Hold it right there. How do you know that?"

"Haven't you heard white tots relish in calling you a nigger?"

"Er, yes...."

"Haven't you seen the photos of white people in Ebony magazine attending lynchings as if they were sporting events?"

"Yeah. So?"

"In the same photos, didn't you see white children at lynchings grinning with their parents?"

Rubbing my stubble, I paused and glanced at my luminous dial military watch–it said 0002. Presently, I said, "Come to think of it, I did. I was so furious and focused on the poor lynched man that I didn't notice the white children standing about. Damn.

There it was in my face and I missed it."

"Do you remember who most of protesters were at Central High in Little Rock?"

"White teens. You're making me see stuff from back then that went right past my head. Shit. The more I think about it, the more hopeless this thing looks...." I took a step toward our dormitories and motioned for Bill to walk with me. "I think I understand Sam Cooke better tonight. In 'Change is Gonna Com,' Sam said, 'It's been too hard living.' Back in the World, that's how I felt every time I set foot off an Air Force base or out of my neighborhood in Madison. It's 'hard living' while at every turn, whites are denying or blocking all avenues to making an adequate living and educating our next generation."

"Amen. But as Sam said, 'change will come.' But it will take time. That may be painful to hear, but, don't give up hope, little brother." Bill gestured toward the Moon, which now looked as if it rested on the horizon. "Our grandfathers and great-grandfathers looked at the same Moon and had conversations similar to the one we're having tonight. They didn't give up hope."

Nodding, I said, "I'm like Nina and Malcom. I'm tired of waiting. Wait for what? What will be different next year?"

"Oh, I don't say wait. I agree. We've done a helluva lotta waitin' already. I mean change will be gradual and take a lot longer than I have patience for. But that's how I see the future unfolding."

My thoughts were interrupted by shouts of "I'm short! Sixteen mo' days and a wakeup! I'm short!" The shouts came from a captain dancing in the street and holding a bottle of wine by its neck. As we moved closer, I saw two lieutenants lying in the middle of the street. One was waving a bottle over his head, saying "Lebun mo' days! I'm better than short. I'm short, short, short!" They began shouting in unison louder than the captain, "I'm short, short!"

A pair of Air Policemen (enlisted men) arrived in a jeep. One stepped out and pleaded with the two officers to get up and not block traffic. They ignored the policeman and continued shouting and singing.

Chuck and Denver arrived beside us from the club. In a split second, Bill was no longer at my flank. Hands akimbo, he had advanced and stood over the celebrating officers and without raising his stern voice, Bill said, "You ignorant sonsabitches are disgraces to your uniforms. Get yo' drunk asses up and off the street. Now!" Bill pointed toward the dormitory. Then, Captain Bill Cobb turned to the celebrating captain.

"And, you, captain, why the hell haven't you taken charge?" The captain's jaw went slack. Bill did not let him respond. "Never fuckin' mind. I don't wanna hear yo' shit. You get the fuck off the street, too."

The three white officers retreated, muttering, "Yes, sir."

Boldness, we had come to expect from Bill Cobb. We knew he had brass balls. Senior and junior officers at Danang Air Base had unfathomable respect for Captain Bill Cobb. But this attitude on deportment was one I never expected from unconventional Bill.

I said, "Wow! I don't know them, but I'm almost sure they know you as the flamboyant dapper captain and F-4 jock. That much is clear, since, as you see, they tucked their tails as if you were a colonel."

Unfazed by my praise, Bill was getting a last look at the top edge of the disappearing Moon. "A man connected to me by whatever means, white or black, who has no self-respect, reflects poorly on me."

Chuck said, "The Air Force is losing big time by letting you go."

In unison, Denver and I said, "Amen."

Bill remained quiet and focused on the Moon.

We were silent for at least a minute, realizing that we were standing with an exemplary fighter pilot, an awesome leader, and a trend-setter that the Air Force didn't think was a 'good fit'.

In a blink, I remembered two other age-group exemplary kinds of guys and leaders from back home in Madison. One was Fernand; the other was my old friend, Virgil. Years before, Virgil and I agreed we had a for real dude in Fernand Hammonds. Though Fernand was somewhat older, it wasn't by much. He didn't seem older just because we were still in high school and he had done a hitch in the army and was attending Alabama A&M on G. I. benefits for veterans.

Back then, Virgil and I played baseball every summer. Fernand was our player-coach-manager. Our team played several teams with players bigger, faster, and more skilled than we were. That didn't matter to Fernand. He played with the all-out zeal and hustle of a Jackie Robinson. No matter the odds, Fernand demonstrated courage and gusto alongside his remarkable skills. We learned more than baseball fundamentals from him. He taught us devotion to duty, and we played hard for each other and for love of the game.

(Following their father's leadership and teaching, years later, two of Fernand's sons played professional baseball. Reggie, the older son whose career ended early due to injury, played in the Pirates' organization. Fernand's younger son, Jeffery, was drafted in 1993 by the Orioles and played in the majors for thirteen years with the Orioles, Reds, Rockies, Brewers, Giants, and Nationals.)

Fernand was also our Boy Scout troop leader. Again, he performed like a team member, leading the way. Virgil and I knew for sure we had the real deal in Fernand when he left his classes at Alabama A&M to help our troop come from behind in a multi-activity competition with boys from a city troop. With Fernand's help, we pulled even with the city dwellers.

The second guy was Virgil, my childhood chum. Virgil was with me the 1965 summer night when I did the most foolish deed of my life. I had graduated from

Tennessee State the month before. We had just left our favorite haunt, the Ebony Club at "the bottom" in Madison, with two other guys because we thought things were "slow." So our party-seeking foursome headed to Decatur in my hot new '65 Pontiac GTO. That car had TriPower carburetors (three two-barrel carburetors) and a 389 cubic inch engine with 360 horsepower. A new Cadillac, occupied by two young white men, pulled beside but did not pass. The guy in the Cadillac's front passenger seat held up a .38 caliber revolver.

Feeling a testosterone surge, I told Roy, my front seat passenger, to show the men in the Cadillac that we had a revolver, too. After seeing that we had a gun and were not afraid, the driver of the Cadillac tried to pull away. I accelerated and refused to let the Cadillac pass. Into the night, we raced along the highway until I had the presence of mind to understand that if the Cadillac passenger fired at us, I would be his first target. I was no infantry expert, but I was convinced that I would die first, then crash and potentially kill all my passengers. I slowed and let the Cadillac go.

The next day, Virgil let me know what he thought. *We were blessed that nothing happened last night. Our lives would have been ruined if we had wounded or, God forbid, killed a white man. We would have faced execution or life imprisonment. You disappointed me; I expected better judgement from you, a college grad. What the hell did they teach you in that college? You don't seem to have learned much. College grad my ass. Besides, what the fuck do you think we could do with*

*your little puny ass .22 caliber against a .38? I guess
you see now that you endangered the lives of all of us.
Don't forget this little talk.* I did not forget Virgil's
little talk.

Standing with Bill that night, I filed him alongside
Fernand and Virgil in my memory as an peer-group
example of real manhood.

Breaking the silence, I said, "Bill, I never hinted
this before, but I want you to know that your bearing,
tone, and character have been a positive influence on
me."

The chorus said, "Me, too."

Bill said, "Thanks, guys." Then he changed the
subject. "Now with Dr. King, Malcom, and Stokely
gone, which path are we likely to take?"

Stunned, I blurted, "What happened to Stokely?
How did he die? When?"

Denver laughed. "Stokely ain't dead. It looks like
he's quitting the Panthers. A couple o' weeks ago, he
just up and moved to Guinea."

"Well, well, what next? And, pray tell, where the
hell is Guinea?"

Bill said, "What the fuck? Don't you know
anything 'bout where we came from? Guinea is in
West Africa. She shares borders with, among others,
Sierra Leone and Liberia."

We had reached Bill and Chuck's dorm. I said, "I
didn't have much to say tonight; so I listened. I don't
know the answers to America's multitudinous
problems, or how we get from here to yonder, but
here's how I see things. Dr. King exemplified real

leadership and was a catalyst for positive change. The changes he helped bring about constitute a start and a direction. Plus, he had it right when he came out against this God-awful war.

"In another sense, James Brown's 'I'm Black and I'm Proud' is a necessary reminder to move away from Euro-centric ideas of beauty and embrace the love of one's kind embodied in the works of Langston Hughes."

Chuck asked, "What about James Baldwin?"

"I have to admit, I don't know enough about Baldwin to comment."

Bill said, "Look, guys, it's morning already and I've got a 0400 brief. We ain't gonna solve this thing tonight–or among us, ever; even if we had years to talk and plan. But there's one thing I wanna get cleared up before I forget again to ask. Carl, where did you get your frequent refrain of here to yonder?"

"Oh, that came from Langston Hughes. My stepfather often quoted Mr. Hughes' 1940s column in the *Chicago Defender*. In particular, my stepfather liked Hughes' character, Jesse B. Semple, who appeared in the column representing the point of view of the common black man. The column was called '*Here to Yonder*.'"

Part Three: Home Again

Chapter 8:
Seeing America

Astronauts Buzz, Neil, and Mike were still all the buzz when my commercial airline flight from Cam Ranh Bay, Vietnam touched down in Seattle, Washington on Monday, July 28, 1969–exactly one year after my departure from these United States. Four days prior, the trio of Apollo XI astronauts had returned from man's first visit to the Moon and landed in the Pacific Ocean. During my homeward journey across the Pacific, Buzz, Neil, and Mike were still in isolation for fear of lunar germs. It seemed much longer than a year had passed since I left for Vietnam following the murders, three months apart, of two iconic Americans–Dr. Martin Luther King and presidential candidate, Robert F. Kennedy.

In the euphoria of my landing on American soil, I knelt and kissed the ground and gave thanks to God for my life and my safe return. Observing my scene at the airport, one would think *I* had been to the Moon. But my priority was to get home to Mama. Within hours, I boarded flights that delivered me to Madison, Alabama and Mama. Another long held dream was fulfilled as I devoured my favorite meal prepared by Mama's hands–turnip greens, black-eyed peas, smothered chicken, rice and cornbread. For a fact, I was home at last!

* * *

The realization of another dream, that I hatched while wide-awake in Vietnam, came after spending many happy days with Mama. A new full-featured burgundy Corvette Stingray with a 427 cubic inch / 435 horsepower engine that I had ordered while still at Danang was ready and waiting for me in Atlanta. While waiting at the dealership for completion of the final new-car prep, others admired my Corvette.

Among the admirers was an Atlanta man about my age whose name I don't remember. So I'll call him Richard. His car was in for maintenance. While we waited, Richard said, "Man, your spectacular new boat's gonna make heads turn and the gals swoon. That's one helluva good lookin' autiemobile."

Though I tried to suppress it, I feel a big grin blossom across my face as I said, "Thank you."

"Say, weren't you in the Booker T. Class o' '61?"

"No. What's a 'Booker T. class'?"

"Uh-huh. You must not be from around here. Booker T. is Booker T. Washington High School. I was in the class o' '63. But, I swear, you could pass for a brother of this little cat who played shortstop for Booker T. back in the day."

As usual, I winced at being called little—even indirectly. But I held my tongue. I shook my head. "No, I'm not from Atlanta. I went to school and played my baseball in Madison, Alabama. I'm just here this afternoon to pick up my car."

"Oh, so what do you do in Madison?"

"Nothing. Madison is where my parents live. I'm an Air Force pilot."

Richard's eyes grew. "Wow! "No shit?"

"Yep. No shit."

"Do you fly them supersonic jet fighters?"

"No. I fly big birds."

"Well, even so, I guess you'll still have to go to Vietnam."

"Actually, I just returned from Nam at the end of July."

Grinning, Richard said, "Wow! So how does it feel to be back in the land o' the free and the home of the brave?"

I turned in my chair to look directly into Richard's face and sized him up. I may have added two plus two and gotten five when the correct answer very well ought to have been three. Presently, after glancing over my shoulder, I lowered my voice and said, "As far as I know, this is the home of the Atlanta Braves and the land of *free,* but only for white folks."

Again, Richard's eyes widened. I saw him inhale. He, too, lowered his voice, nodded and said, "Right on, brother man. Right on."

With that response, I thought he sounded a lot like my friend, Bee Settles.

Returning to my original sitting posture, I resumed reading a sports magazine, passing time before I could drive my new car. In an article, the Braves and Dodgers caught my attention. The pennant race in the National League's new Western Division was hot. Five teams fighting for the lead and were within two games of each other. Included among the five leaders were the Braves and Dodgers.

Richard interrupted my reading by announcing, "Say, Brother Carl, there ain't much daylight left. Since this is yo' first time in Atlanta, don't you think it's a bit late to be starting for Madison over unfamiliar roads?"

Checking my watching and stretching, I said, "Yeah, you're right."

"Why don't you stay over and tonight go with me to the hottest club in town."

Interested, I dropped the magazine. "Tell me more."

"Well, it's new and is still all the rage 'round these parts, near and far. It's called the Pink Pussycat."

Laughing, I said, "The pink *what*?"

Grinning, Richard said, "Yeah, you heard right. The Pink Pussycat. I hear plenty o' single women are there every night of the week."

"Now, you're talkin'. Not that I'd know after you tell me, but where is it?"

"Oh, it ain't far. It's over on Simpson Road. But never mind directions. You can follow me."

First, we caravanned to Richard's apartment. Before getting his shower, he opened a jar and took out a marijuana joint. After taking two puffs, he held it out to me. "Here, have a drag."

Now that I was back in the States (or back in World, as we would say in 'Nam) and feeling invincible, I felt no fear. I thought *Vietnam didn't kill me. So, what the hell, I'm ready to try anything–at least once.*

Cautiously, I took the joint. While I was looking at it, Richard disappeared to take his shower. Finally, I took a puff. After the second puff, my head felt strange. Immediately, I became fearful and paranoid. The walls seemed to close in on me. Then I decided I had better forget the Pink Pussycat and escape from Richard while he showered.

I didn't know where I was or where I was going. But I felt I had to get away. I found my car and quickly left the parking lot. I told myself *just keep driving.* I had the sensation of traveling really fast–perhaps, a hundred miles per hour. I didn't want a ticket, but when I checked the speedometer, it showed only thirty miles per hour. Drivers behind me were honking. One passed me and said, "Why did you buy a Corvette if you can't drive it?"

The first motel I saw was where I decided to spend the night. It didn't matter what condition the place was in, I had to stop driving. After checking in, my first stop was the motel's restaurant. When my grilled chicken breast, rice, gravy, and green beans arrived, matters in my head went from strange to weird. When I tried to cut the chicken, I thought it moved! The more I tried to cut the chicken, the more aggressive it seemed. I decided the chicken was fighting me. But I was determined to show the chicken who was master. My moves to defeat the chicken drew unwanted attention.

Someone called the manager. He told me, "Young man, if you don't like the food, I'll give you your money back. Your bizarre behavior is causing a scene and scaring my customers. So I'm asking you to please leave before I call the police."

I had no place to go but to my room. I was damn sure not about to try driving again. I promised myself that if I lived through the night, I would never smoke marijuana again. I spent a long night walking back and forth in my room until I finally slept sometime not long before dawn.

When I awoke, my paranoia was gone. I thanked God for taking care of me in my time of trouble and preventing me from demolishing my new Corvette. Back home in Madison, I told a friend my marijuana story. He said, "Your marijuana was probably laced with PCP or some other chemicals that made you paranoid and hallucinate."

* * *

Too soon, my vacation was over and it was time to report for my first post-Vietnam duty at Castle Air Force Base near Merced, California. En route, I planned to visit with my college classmate and Vietnam buddy, Fig Newton, at his new duty station, George Air Force Base near Victorville, California.

This was an opportunity to see the United States along the famous Route Sixty-six (a highway designated U. S. 66) from near the middle of the country to California. My last vacation hours were spent in Memphis, Tennessee with college chums. On a sunny August morning, I rolled onto U. S. 40 and headed west across the mile-long Memphis-Arkansas

Memorial Bridge at an altitude of more than one-hundred feet above the Mississippi River. To my right were two railroad bridges. As the day passed, I learned that I would drive beside railroads much of the time on my 'big cross-country adventure.'

The first day went as planned. Twelve hours or so out of Memphis and bone-tired after crossing Arkansas and Oklahoma, I checked into a motel in Amarillo, Texas. In Amarillo, a series of small troubles began.

The next morning, I overslept. In haste, I packed and made my way to Route 66. All I had time to see in Amarillo were highway signs and a bite to eat. Little more than a hundred miles west of Amarillo, I stopped for gasoline in a tiny three gas station town called Glenrio–half in Texas and half in New Mexico. In Glenrio, I discovered that in my great hurry, I had left my wallet at the motel. The wallet contained six one-hundred dollar bills and my driver's license. But I could pay for the gasoline out of the small bills I had in my pocket.

After finding the number on the motel receipt, I called the manager. "Good morning, again. This is Carl…."

She cut me off. "Ah, yes, Mr. Gamble. I've been expecting your call. You want to know about your wallet, don't you?"

Ecstatic that something was going right, I said, "Yes, yes!"

Before I could say more the manager said, "Well, don't worry. A maid gave it to me."

At the word 'worry', I went from ecstatic to really worried. Kneading my forehead between beads of perspiration, I said, "Is there any money in it?"

"Let's see." Pause. "Yes, I see six one-hundred dollar bills."

Ecstatic again, I took a deep breath and thought *there are some good people left in the world.* "That's great! Please give the maid fifty dollars and you keep fifty."

"Humph! I will do no such thing." She paused, then said, "Okay. Well, partially. I'll do as you ask and give the maid fifty, but I will not take a penny for me."

Flabbergasted, all I could think to say was, "Okay. Thank you, ma'am."

"All right. Now, let's figure out how to get you on your way."

It took only a few minutes of work to devise a plan that would keep me moving westward. First, the Amarillo motel manager would arrange with her mother-in-law to lend me one-hundred dollars. Her mother-in-law, Ms. Lillian Redman, was managing the Blue Swallow Motel in the small town of Tucumcari, New Mexico. Ms. Redman's motel, made of fourteen stand-alone units, was an hour's drive to the west of my gasoline stop. The Amarillo motel manager also promised to mail my wallet and four-hundred fifty dollars to Fig. I thought *though I screw up repeatedly, God, you're still good to me.*

In Tucumcari, Ms. Redman greeted me at the door of her office/residence unit with, "Are you the little colored boy looking for the money?"

I heard "little colored boy." I felt the usual visceral response in my head and stomach. My face felt tight as I tried to smile and talk. "Yes, ma'am. I'm the little colored boy looking for the money."

By the time I was back in my car, the "little colored boy" bit had fallen from me and lay on sandy soil of the Great Chihuahan Desert. All I allowed to matter was new found contentment now that I had enough money for one more night in a motel at Flagstaff, Arizona, gasoline, and food. I was ready again to take a satisfied smile on the road and enjoy my trip.

My smiles ended less than sixty miles later when I saw police lights flashing in my rearview mirror. Because I did not have my license with me, I had made sure not to speed. I stopped on the shoulder of U. S. 66.

A stern-faced New Mexico highway patrolman marched to my open window. "Boy, lemme see your license and registration."

"Yes, sir, officer." While reaching for my registration, I asked. "Is there something wrong? Are you citing me for some infraction?"

"A Corvette like this one was reported stolen. I need to make sure this isn't the one."

I handed over my registration and said, "Officer, I apologize, but in my hurry to leave my motel in Amarillo this morning, I left my wallet and driver's license behind."

After hearing this news, the demeanor of New Mexico's finest went from condescending to belligerent. Stepping back from my door and with one hand on his weapon, he said, "Okay, boy. So you think I was born yesterday. You lying nigger, get your sorry ass outta the car–s*lowly*–and put your hands behind your back."

Handcuffed, I stood beside my car while he said, "Boy, you stole this car. I know it, 'cause ain't no nigger yo' age make enough money to buy no car like this."

I thought, *There will be no point to argue with a white man, especially one who has a gun, out here in the middle of a desert with no one around. I haven't seen but three cars all morning....*

I remained silent.

Without a warrant or probable cause, he proceeded to search my car. He opened everything and saw my military orders and dog tags. He could not and would not believe I was the Air Force captain in the orders. Finally, he announced, "I'ma hafta lock you up until I verify who owns this car. I'll have it towed to town."

At the jail in Santa Rosa, I was permitted one phone call. I called the motel manager in Amarillo. "Ma'am, I'm sorry to bother you again. But would you tell this highway patrolman what's on my driver's license?"

Meanwhile, I was locked in a cell with people vomiting or peeing on themselves. All the while, amid the stench, drunks slept off their over indulgence. Standing in the cell, I thought about what could have been a nightmare-ending to an incident a few years before in Alabama. Gripping the bars with both hands,

I realized this was a minor inconvenience compared to the disaster that could have occurred that night on a highway between four black guys armed with a .22, and two white guys carrying a .38. Jail time might well have been holding time until execution.

Releasing the bars and hitting a fist into my palm, I thought *Man, what the hell were we thinking?* I shuddered at the memory and hunched my shoulders to calm myself.

The Santa Rosa jail was a horrible place. Worse, it brought back an abysmal memory.

When the officer received my license number and authenticated it with Alabama authorities, he released me. He also gave me a printed note with my license information in case I was stopped again. "Okay, you're free to go. Oh, yeah. About the tow; no charge."

All I could do was seethe inside and be silent.

No apology; no paperwork–nothing. For him, this incident never happened.

Two evenings later, I arrived at George Air Force Base and visited with Fig and his family. I was no fun. All I wanted to do was sleep.

Chapter 9:
Cold Warrior

"Dammit! Sonavabitch!"

My hand stung from the force I used to slam my orders onto my desk. Near the end of my tour of duty in Vietnam, I learned that I had been assigned to fly for the Air Force's Strategic Air Command (SAC) when I returned to the States. I would rather have been hit with a hammer than fly for SAC. Amazing stories were told by former SAC B-52 pilots Skip Woodward and Bill Walsh in the dormitories and at the Officer's Club during our Danang days about SAC crews on alert duty fourteen days per month at their stateside bases. Plus, they were deployed repeatedly to Southeast Asia for combat duty over Vietnam for three or six months at a time. I wanted no part of that life.

SAC's mission, beginning in 1946, was "be prepared to conduct long-range offensive operations in any part of the world...." Succinctly and directly put, in 1969, SAC was responsible for delivering immediate and devastating nuclear retaliation against our primary Cold War adversary, the Soviet Union. SAC's main tools to accomplish this mission in 1969 were the B-52 long-range bomber and the KC-135 aerial refueling tanker. Midair refueling significantly extended the range of the B-52. The B-52 was famous, but not the KC-135. Aerial refueling from KC-135s enabled B-52s to deliver nuclear weapons to anywhere on the planet.

Regular drills and training flights were conducted to ensure liftoff within minutes after the alert horn sounded. Meeting this rigid requirement meant that SAC's strike force would be airborne before its bases could be destroyed by enemy nuclear weapons. B-52 and KC-135 crews would learn whether or not it was the "real thing" only after they taxied to the runway.

To achieve the fastest possible response, crews on alert duty had to stay together around the clock for seven consecutive days twice a month. The crews hung out together in what they affectionately called their "alert shack" reading, sleeping, playing board games, playing cards, watching TV, or otherwise being bored. Little wonder that the divorce rates for SAC personnel were among the highest in the military.

* * *

En route to Castle Air Force Base, California, I was still trying my best to think of a way out of my assignment to SAC.

Upon requesting a date of separation to leave the Air Force at Castle Air Force Base, I was given what I thought was the runaround when told that I must apply at my permanent duty station, K. I. Sawyer Air Force Base. Personnel at Castle knew, and I knew, that once I reported to K. I. Sawyer Air Force Base on Michigan's upper-peninsula, a SAC base, they would never let me go. Besides, my KC-135 training at Castle would add four more years to my military obligation.

Dejected and beyond disgusted, I thought, *I'm fucked. I never liked the idea of a SAC assignment because of alert duty. How did I get the very assignment that I wanted no part of?*

Oh, well. I guess I'll have to find a way to live with it. Sorry, Lord, for my piss-poor attitude. Please forgive me.

Sitting in the classroom alone before the first session, I made a resigned sigh and thought; *I should never dillydally when deciding. While still in Danang, I had all the input I needed to decide whether to stay in the Air Force or leave. My bad. So suck it up, dude, and deal with it.*

The similarities between the KC-135 tanker and the commercial jet airliner 707 became my focus. I had to find a silver lining for what appeared to be a dark cloud over my flying career. My silver lining turned out to be the KC-135.

The KC-135 and 707 were derivatives in the mid-twentieth century from the same mother, the 1954 hand-built sleek swept-wing four jet engine Boeing 367-80. She rolled out of the factory three days before the Supreme Court decided Brown v. Board of Education. This solitary research airplane was known to insiders at Boeing as the "Dash 80." Several years before, I had been impressed as a passenger during a flight aboard an American Airlines 707. While I was an Air Force ROTC cadet, I was made as happy as a pig in mud when given the rare opportunity to maneuver a KC-135 already inflight. She flew like a dream. That sealed the deal; I was in love. The sisters were revolutionary airplanes; the first military jet transport and tanker and the premier jet airliner in the worldwide airline industry. Though they are of the same design and looked like copies of each other, or twins, their measurements are different.

(Today, the Dash 80 is called one of the twelve most important airplanes ever built and is housed in the Smithsonian National Air and Space Museum's facility at Washington Dulles International Airport.)

* * *

Thirteen weeks later, on a balmy day in mid-November 1969, I departed Castle Air Force Base as a certified KC-135 copilot. I left behind my old friend from Danang days, Bee Settles, who had arrived to join a subsequent KC-135 class. During my stay at Castle, I met a new friend, C. J. Hayes, a B-52 pilot. Bee and C. J. are among my lifelong friends.

My journey from Castle to K. I. Sawyer Air Force Base took me and my Corvette through Denver and Detroit. The highlight of my stopover in Denver was a visit with another Danang buddy, Alex Dawson. We sipped our favorite beverages and reminisced about our adventures in Vietnam and Australia.

With my third shot of Jack Daniels in-hand, I said, "It seems each time we tell our stories the more they resemble fish stories."

"How's that, ol' partner?"

"They grow and become more incredible every time!"

* * *

Mississippi Delta people migrated to Chicago. Many Madison residents and folks from surrounding communities migrated to Detroit. My neighbors, from near and far, had an affinity for Detroit. Hoping to soak up some home grown culture, I made this my next stop.

My drive from Detroit to K. I. Sawyer was north, and then west. The temperature dropped more and more as the miles piled up. Eight hours and four-hundred fifty-five miles later, I arrived at the base and learned that the snow I saw was not an anomaly.

The duty officer at the 46th Air Refueling Squadron's headquarters building had a friendly chat with me as I signed in.

"Like me, you must be from down South. I arrived here summer before last and was shocked when snowfall started in mid-November."

Wide-eyed, all I could say was, "Wow!"

Laughing, he said, "Wait. There's more. In some years, you can expect more than a foot of snow to hide the ground into May."

My Madison, Alabama sensibilities shivered. "Why, my God, the ground's not uncovered long enough to fit a whole baseball season."

The duty officer laughed so hard that he fell back into his chair. When he recovered, he said, "What's more, the temperature dropping to minus twenty degrees ain't unusual at all." He laughed again. "That's why quarters here have electrical outlets where you can plug in your car to keep the engine block warm overnight; otherwise, your cute lil' Corvette ain't gonna start. Welcome to K. I. Sawyer."

* * *

My duties as a KC-135 copilot meant, as one would expect, that I occasionally flew the airplane. I was also the operator of the fuel transfer pumps during aerial refueling. Contrary to popular belief, the KC-135 boom operator does not "pump fuel." Chief among the reasons that fuel transfer is a task performed by a pilot is that the center of gravity changes in the airplane when fuel is dispensed from one tank or another. If not controlled with the airplane's trim in mind, the result could cause the loss of two or more airplanes and crews. An out of balance weight situation could pitch the nose or tail up or down and end in catastrophe.

Like all KC-135 crews, the team I joined before Christmas in 1969 practiced our craft of refueling B-52s miles above the Earth and at speeds of hundreds of miles per hour. Within a single mission, several simultaneous refuelings could be in operation simultaneously. I loved this job, but still hated "alert duty" with passion.

* * *

March rolled in on a howling blizzard. Two weeks later, an even bigger one was forecast. While in the commissary stocking my shopping cart with food for the coming blizzard, I heard a voice say, "Young man. Yes, you with that teeming cart. You must have many mouths to feed at your house."

I turned and recognized the only black lieutenant colonel at K. I. Sawyer. Both of us were dressed in civvies. I remembered him from his introduction by the wing commander upon arrival a few weeks before. Grinning, I said, "Oh, no sir. It's all for me. The pantry is empty and I'm still a growing boy."

He gave a toothy smile and extended his hand, "I'm Joe Blaylock. How are you?"

Immediately, I liked him. He never mentioned his rank. A friendship ensued in which I never felt like the junior partner, though I referred to him as "Colonel Blaylock." My deference was natural, for it came from my Alabama raising and military tradition–both based on respect for one's elders.

The next time I saw Colonel Blaylock was during one of my stints on alert duty. Again, our encounter was warm and pleasant. Though I did not ask, I thought, *Why the hell is a lieutenant colonel on alert duty as a pilot?* I had not seen a pilot or navigator above the rank of major on alert duty.

Over time, we became better acquainted and our friendship grew. During a slow walk on a bright sunny day outside the "alert shack," that did not look at all like an Alabama shack that I ever saw, I asked, "Sir, do you really like pulling on alert duty?"

Colonel Blaylock stopped in his tracks and glanced over his shoulders. No one was nearby. "No. Carl, I dislike alert duty as much as the next man. It wreaks havoc on husbands and wives and I suspect alert duty may also cause unseen damage in children. But the answer to your question requires some background for context that you cannot repeat."

Standing beside me, he raised an eyebrow and slowly turned to face me directly without losing eye contact. I felt the gravity of the importance of words he would speak before he spoke. Not sure I wanted to hear; I nodded and said, "Sir, I will hold anything you share with me in strict confidence."

Almost imperceptibly, he nodded. Colonel Blaylock said, "There aren't many black squadron commanders around. I agreed to come to K. I. Sawyer because I thought I had an understanding, a so-called gentlemen's agreement, that I would become the commanding officer of the 46th."

I felt my eyes grow. All I could think to say was, "Well, sir, can it still happen?"

"Right now, I have less than a snowball's chance in hell to get command of the 46th."

"But sir…."

He cut me off. "Carl, forget the promise of command. I have."

Shaking my head, I said, "But sir, I don't understand how this could happen."

Colonel Blaylock grimaced. "Well, Carl, I know you've heard of the 'good old boys' network. I assure you; such networks live within the Air Force. Someone at the Pentagon, who can change the minds of mere personnel officers who made promises to me, may have made different promises to a friend. I can see this especially being true when someone up there decides to reward one of his boys with a squadron commander's job."

"But that's not fair. What about equal opportunity?"

He shook his head. "Sad but true, Carl. Life is not always fair. I know you see that we were born into a country where white skin pretty much guarantees privilege. Today, if the competition is black, there is no need for a 'tiebreaker.' When the competition is between two whites, the tiebreakers become class, political influencers, and other even less visible means of prevailing.

"So, no matter recent legislation, our chances at high achievement in or outside the Air Force will remain slim and the odds high."

Colonel Blaylock reached out and laid a hand on my shoulder. "Don't despair. Don't let'em get you down. Remember. Timing is everything. That was especially true for three-star General Benjamin O. Davis, Jr. Like General Davis, you're a skilled pilot. Unlike General Davis, it was not your lot to be a fighter ace and win a Silver Star. Nonetheless, opportunities for you may still come in the Air Force or outside of the Air Force in the airline business. Keep your chin up. They can't take away your drive or your dignity."

"But sir, what will *you* do?"

He actually smiled. "Don't worry. I'll retire in a few months and land on my feet."

Despite the bad hand dealt to Colonel Blaylock, he held his head up and did not become bitter. My friend, Joe Blaylock, made a memorable impression on me.

* * *

Nine months after happily leaving Vietnam, I was back in Southeast Asia participating in the Vietnam War, but this time based at U-Tapao Air Base in Thailand. Our entire KC-135 crew of four (pilot/aircraft commander, copilot, navigator, and boom operator) deployed with the same orders as other crews: For ninety days, fly aerial refueling missions for the 307th Strategic Wing in primary support of their B-52s in *Operation Arc Light* against targets in Cambodia, Laos, and South Vietnam. Second, we were to aerial refuel tactical aircraft. Many B-52 crews flying ninety-day stints for the 307th SW were scavenged from stateside SAC bases as was KC-135 crews. Stateside KC-135 crews flying for the 307th were known as "Young Tigers."

Several crews flew deadhead with us in the back of a KC-135 flown by a crew from another stateside SAC base on a circuitous route to Thailand. After two days of briefings and administrative details, our crew flew our first mission to refuel B-52s bound for targets along the Ho Chi Minh Trail just inside the Laotian border. On takeoff in the warm humid tropical air, the KC-135 my crew flew used nearly the entire eleven-thousand-foot runway. Through the windshield, I saw more details in the perimeter fence beyond the end of the runway than I ever needed to know. I felt the ol' pucker string relax as we cleared the fence.

Our B-52 receivers from Andersen AFB on Guam found us waiting in our refueling track, this time, over the Gulf of Tonkin. The planned refueling was textbook and done with precision and a minimum of radio chatter. Looking back at it from today, I am still amazed at how we made the dangerous operation of fuel transfer between two large airplanes traveling at more than three-hundred miles per hour, one of which was carrying twenty-eight tons of bombs, almost routine. This was our routine for three months at U-Tapao Air Base.

Near the end of June, we departed the hot war in Southeast Asia and within days we were back at K. I. Sawyer on the dreaded alert duty, having rejoined the Cold War.

* * *

Colonel Blaylock met me at the Officer's Club for lunch. "Hey, Carl, welcome back. How was it?"

"Thanks. It was war from thirty-thousand feet and for the most part, out of harm's way."

"Hey, you're back. Why the long face?"

"Oh, I guess because the war appears no closer to an end than it did a year ago when I was there. Too many people are dying for reasons I don't understand."

He took a deep breath and said, "Markets, my man, greed, markets, and money drive the cause of most wars. It can even prolong wars. Now that we've cleared up that mystery, what else is on your mind?"

I leaned in and whispered. "Is it true? Are we bombing in Cambodia?"

"Yes. I heard it from a B-52 navigator who flew out of Kadena."

"Well, how can he be sure?"

"It pisses me off that the folks in Washington think we're fools. They have some clandestine guys on the ground using MSQ-77 radar to guide B-52 crews to the release point and tell them a precise time to release their bombs. Mind you, all this happens in night raids. Because of that, they think the crews won't know where the bombs landed. Then our brass in Saigon and Washington tell the press that these raids were *Arc Light* strikes inside South Vietnam.

"All the navigators record the coordinates during the drop. One look at a map will show any idiot that the bombs didn't fall on South Vietnam."

I put my elbows on the table and cupped my chin in both hands. "Damn!"

"Let's get off depressing subjects. Let's celebrate your return. Come by the house tonight for dinner. I'll get Newby and his wife to join us. Whatta ya say?"

* * *

Several months later, Colonel Blaylock retired. In less than two weeks after his departure, I decided if the Air Force could treat a lieutenant colonel the way Joe Blaylock was treated, then why not me? I didn't want to wait and see the movie. The trailer was more than enough. I went to personnel and made it official. I got a separation date that coincided with the end of my Air Force obligation, three years to go and out–13 November 1973.

* * *

Summer, 1971, I qualified as a KC-135 aircraft commander. A month after celebrating my new status as aircraft commander, my new crew flew with me to deliver a KC-135 to Carswell Air Force Base near Fort Worth, Texas for heavy maintenance. The trip gave me the opportunity to visit with Colonel Blaylock and Major Newby. Both had chosen Dallas/Fort Worth as their retirement home.

"Hey, Carl, welcome to Dallas!" Colonel Blaylock bounded out his front door and bear-hugged me on the front stoop of his new home while his wife stood beaming in the doorway. Only a year had passed since they left K. I. Sawyer, but his new neighbors may have concluded that we had been separated since childhood.

After dinner, drinks in hand, we sat by the pool as Major Newby and Colonel Blaylock told house-hunting and house-building stories. I wanted to change the subject to golf. "So Colonel Blaylock...."

Holding a hand up, he cut me off. "Carl, my friend, you've gotta try harder to stop calling me colonel. I'm just plain ol' 'Joe.'"

I almost said, "Yes, sir." But I held my tongue. Grinning, I sipped my Jack Daniels and said, "So Joe how's your golf game now that you have several more months per year to practice and play here in Texas?"

"Very funny. And I might add, very well, thank you."

"Have you been taking lessons from your young cousin?"

"Who?"

"You know, your cousin Jane."

Joe frowned then burst into laughter."

Newby was puzzled. "Who the hell is Jane?"

Joe explained. "Jane Blalock is the twenty-something Ladies Professional Golf Association rookie of the year from a couple of years ago. She's become a star."

Newby shrugged and said, "So?"

Blaylock laughed and slapped his knee. "So she's white, that's what. And I don't think she's my cousin. Oh, yes, neither does Carl, sitting here grinning like a Cheshire cat. By the way, Newby, speaking of white, tell Carl about the white neighbor who interrupted your lawn work."

Now, Newby laughed. He took another drag on his stubby Tiparillo. "Yeah, Carl, the week after we moved in, I was out manicuring my front lawn. Since this lawn is *really* mine and not property of the US Air Force, I don't mind putting in extra effort for a great result." Newby dusted his Tiparillo and sipped his rum and Coke. "Well, I knew I was doing a yeoman's job, but had not realized how good it was until a neighbor stopped his car and called me to the street. He complimented my workmanship and asked me how much I was charging 'to do this lawn.' At first, I was confused. Then, it hit me. I knew damned well he couldn't be asking me what I finally figured he was asking. So to be clear, I asked him, 'are you asking me how much I am paid to cut this yard?' When he said, yes, I thought my temples would burst. My heart was pounding. I had not been that angry in years. I pointed to my house and said, 'The lady who lives there pays me very well. She lets me sleep with her!'"

* * *

Back at K. I. Sawyer, summer seemed to "pass go" and slid directly into the long winter. My three crewmen glided comfortably into a smooth operating team. First Lieutenant Steve Coleman was my copilot and Captain William Kilgore was navigator. Technical Sergeant Edgar Boatright operated the boom.

We were aloft on a heading of 093 at thirty-thousand feet and about to finish a routine training mission over Northern Minnesota about 1230, Friday, 11 February 1972 when I heard on the radio, "Badger 21, this is Charlie Papa. Go to channel 17.2 for a mission. Over."

Puzzled, Steve and I glanced at each other. This was unusual. I said, "This is Badger 21, roger, out." On channel 17.2, I keyed my mic and said, "CP, this Badger 21. Ready for mission. Over."

"Badger 21, Situation: four fishermen are adrift on an ice floe on Lake Superior near Copper Harbor. Locals estimate the floe will drift southeast, melting as it goes, water temperature approximately thirty-seven degrees Foxtrot. Hypothermia will render a man unconscious in 15-18 minutes at said temperature. Mission: immediately terminate training assignment, and proceed to vicinity of Copper Harbor, descend to ten-thousand feet, and commence search. Over."

"This is Badger 21, roger. Proceeding to Copper Harbor vicinity. Out."

The entire crew heard the order. On the intercom, I said, "Billy, give me a heading for Copper Harbor."

Billy's response was immediate. He had already mapped our route. "Come to heading 096. That'll put us north of but within sight of the point at Copper Harbor. ETA: 7 minutes at 520 knots."

"Roger, 096."

"Edgar, watch and report."

"Roger, watch and report."

We arrived at Copper Harbor. I said, "Steve, you handle the radio, I've got the airplane. Get permission to descend to five thousand."

"Roger. Five thousand."

"Okay. We'll make a track of left turns and widen the track each time around. Ideas?"

I heard a chorus on the intercom: "Sounds good."

Edgar had the advantage of the best downward and panoramic view of the ground from his perch at his refueling station in the tail of the airplane. Two minutes later, Edgar spoke. "Sir, I see floes and debris on some of them. At five-thousand feet, I'll never be able to say for sure if I see a man."

Steve reminded us. "CP was firm. Don't go lower than five."

I said, "Edgar, how low do we need to go to find these people before they meet catastrophe?"

"I'd say two."

"Billy and Steve, I say we stay off the radio and let's go find these people. I've got the airplane and she's responsive. What do you think?"

Both said, "Let's do it."

"Okay. Here we go." I leveled off at two. At two-thousand feet, there was less I could do to save my crew and the airplane from an error committed by me, wind shear, or aircraft fault. I concentrated on flying. I depended on Steve and Edgar for searching. Billy had no window at his navigator's station. Besides, I needed him to help me avoid overflying the same patch of water twice.

After about thirty minutes of circling, Edgar said, "Bingo! Eight o'clock from my position, mark coordinates."

Billy said, "Roger that! Marked!"

I said, "Steve, standby to report *after* we make a verify pass." Then I turned right for almost 45 degrees and made a big loop to the left to return over the same track without banking the airplane beyond her limits to remain in controlled flight.

"Billy, get me back just north of the track we just flew. I want this pass to be directly over the correct floe."

"Okay, Carl, gotcha. Come left five degrees. Okay hold that. Hold it. Hooollld it. Okay, go back to your original heading. You're damn good! You were almost on it!"

Seated behind me, Billy couldn't see my satisfied smile. It vanished in a split second as I refocused on flying our KC-135 far below any sensible cursing altitude for an airplane that large.

Edgar broke my concentration. "We've got'em! There're four of'em. There're directly below and they're waving their asses off."

147

Billy said, "Marked at 47°20'55.4"N 87°38'29.2"W."

Steve looked at me as I focused on the altimeter dialing up past three-thousand feet.

Without taking my eyes off my instrument panel, I said, "Guys, I'm damn proud of every one of you. You were cool and performed well. Those fishermen and their families will remember your deed for many years. Steve, go ahead and report their coordinates.

"Let's go home."

* * *

Before the end of the month and before the praise at K. I. Sawyer and in the city of Marquette had died for our part in the rescue of the fishermen, my crew and I were Young Tigers again. We were back in Thailand flying KC-135 aerial refueling missions for B-52s and a great variety of tactical aircraft–Air Force, Marines, and Navy fighter jets. The routine sorties we flew for the next five weeks were unremarkable. With only twelve more weeks to go, we would rotate back to K. I. Sawyer before the end of May–and after the snow was gone. I was counting down the days as I did back at Danang in '69. The war was looking better from my point of view. The US Army was withdrawing troops at a rapid pace. President Nixon's "Vietnamization Plan" would soon have us out of Southeast Asia and that was fine with me.

Then, on Easter Sunday, 2 April 1972, North Vietnam began a three-point invasion that changed my mind about the war winding down. Nixon's response to the invasion was late, but resulted in a significant new escalation of the air war. Though the US Army was still withdrawing troops, the air war was hot and getting hotter. Hundreds of bombers and fighters arrived in Southeast Asia during April and May.

Sitting in my quarters listening to Marvin Gaye's "What's going on," I found new meaning in his words. "We don't need to escalate. You see, war is not the answer...." I thought, *Damn, how long can this war drag on?* I shrugged and my musings continued, *A long frigging time is the answer. It's been almost four years since the first time I was over here.* I shook my head as I thought *my real question is 'can my crew and I go home as scheduled by the end of the May?' This blasted war be damned!*

Beginning on 5 April, there was an influx of hundreds of bombers and fighters arriving in Operation Freedom Train. We refueled inbound B-52s deployed to bases in Thailand. By 9 May, Operation Linebacker was launched. This time the B-52s and fighters were flying sorties over North Vietnam in addition to South Vietnam and Laos. This meant that on occasion we took our turn flying refueling tracks for Air Force and Navy fighters over the Gulf of Tonkin between the coast of North Vietnam and the Navy's Yankee Station (carriers and their escorts). Our tanker met receivers, aircraft requiring fuel, aloft at planned Air Refueling Tracks. For fighters, the tracks were multilayered and elliptical. With our receiver taking on fuel, we were separated in the track from other tankers by a thousand feet nose to nose and as few as five-hundred vertical feet, in altitude, as we flew our oval pattern making left turns.

About a week before my crew was to return stateside, we were operating or maneuvering close to the coast of North Vietnam. On a bright and clear day, we were flying the "Purple" refueling track over the Western Gulf of Tonkin and well north of the DMZ. Bomb-laden Navy F-4s and Air Force F-105s had refueled and gone their separate routes to targets in North Vietnam's ports and railyards. We flew our track patterns and waited for their return. As usual, we refueled returning flights of four F-4s that didn't have enough fuel to return to their carriers.

A Navy F-4 flight leader said, "Thanks, guys. That's a save!" He meant we had saved eight crew members and four very expensive airplanes. This day, I heard a Ground Control Interception (GCI) break in over the voice of the Navy pilot. "Young Tiger 21, this is Brigham Charlie Papa, over."

This was the first call I had from Brigham, a GCI control point that directed fighters egressing from North Vietnam to tankers on an as needed basis. After a moment's hesitation, I responded, "This is Young Tiger 21, over."

A calm voice said, "21, this is Brigham. We have an Air Force F-4G damaged by ground fire and leaking fuel from an internal wing tank. He also reports damage to his center drop tank; can't make your station. He's jettisoning the drop tank. Can you go meet him?"

I took a deep breath. This sounded like a flight over North Vietnam in an airplane that was a prime target. We knew KC-135s were considered high value targets by North Vietnamese air defense forces. I said, "This is 21, understand need to meet F-4G off track, over.

"Affirmative."

"Roger, wait."

On our intercom, I said, "Guys, as you may have guessed, this 'meeting' may mean acquiring a receiver just south of the Hanoi Hilton. Are you with me?"

Billy, Steve, and Edgar answered in unison, "Let's do it!"

Billy added, "Let's go bring him home, or at least get his feet wet in friendly waters."

I said, "Okay. Here we go. Billy, grab your air defense charts and be ready."

Billy said, "Roger that! I'm ready."

Rules of engagement prohibited KC-135s from flying over North Vietnam. The rule had been violated many times over the years. Sometimes aircraft commanders were punished by their boss, sometimes not. I had no idea what my boss would say and I was not about to ask. The guy on the "Brigham" call sign at Udorn Air Base in Thailand knew the rules as well as we did. He had made sure his request did not sound like an order.

I keyed my mic. "Brigham, this is 21. We're ready. Vector the intercept."

Brigham's radar displayed the positions of all aircraft flying in the sector–ours and the enemy's.

"Roger. This is Brigham. Thank you. The other 4Gs in the Weasel flight will suppress enemy fire for you."

"This is 21. Thanks. Roger."

"This is Brigham. Come to heading 330, descending to twenty thousand over eleven minutes."

"This is 21. Roger, 330 for eleven at twenty thousand. Out."

On the intercom, Billy said, "Oh, shit! That will put us damn nearly on top of Ninh Binh's antiaircraft fire."

I said, "Okay, Billy. Let's go north and pass Ninh Binh on the gulf side. Then we can hook west, then south and get another vector from Brigham."

"Roger. Come to heading 345."

"Roger. 345."

"Steve, take the radio. I've got the airplane. Tell Brigham what we're doing before he asks why we're off the heading he gave us."

Steve said, "Roger. I've got the radio."

My mind went back to the slow-ass C-47 "bullshit bomber" I flew three years earlier. I felt only slightly more comfortable in my KC-135 moving at five times the speed and more than ten times the altitude. Yet the old pucker string tightened. *Hmmm*, I thought. On the intercom, I said, "Hey Billy, I'm increasing our speed in a twenty degree dive to get us to the hook sooner and take a couple o' minutes off the time we're a target for some hotshot antiaircraft guy. Recalculate as needed."

"Fucking-A! Let's get this damn thing the hell over with!"

In spite of myself, I laughed–so did Steve and Edgar. We made our hook and Steve asked Brigham for a vector update.

"This is Brigham, I see you're early. That's a good thing. Our 4G guy needs you quickly. He guesses less than two minutes fuel. He's preparing to bail. Don't think he can make 'feet wet.' His altitude has dropped to twelve-thousand; airspeed slowed to 480. He's now on this frequency."

I took the radio. "Brigham, this is 21. Here's what we do: give us a vector for refuel that will also work for egress."

"This is Brigham. Roger, wait." Ten seconds later he was back. "Go to 180. Copy? Over."

"Roger, 180 and twelve thousand. Out. Weasel 4, this is Yankee Tango 21. I'm coming in six o'clock high. Will pass over and descend in front of you. Be there in 30-40 seconds. Will that work for you? Over."

"This is 4. Affirmative. Let's do it! Quick! Out."

After flying over the stricken F-4G rear to front, I descended ahead of Weasel 4 to about a hundred feet above his altitude and reduced my speed.

Edgar had Weasel 4 on the boom seconds before his F-4G Phantom flamed out (engine failure for lack of fuel). In 125 seconds, Steve transferred 1,700 gallons of fuel to Weasel 4, filling his internal tanks to about 90% of capacity. I could see the Gulf of Tonkin ahead and to my left. Two minutes later, we were over the gulf but still in enemy territory.

Weasel 4 rolled off station and was flying in formation opposite and trailing my left wing. "Yankee Tango 21, this Weasel 4. Thanks a million! You saved my ass from a stay in the Hanoi Hilton! Over."

Steve said, "This is 21. Roger, you're welcome. Just in case, stay with us on heading 151 to Danang. Over."

"Roger that! I don't know my rate of fuel loss; so, you betcha, I'm staying with you. Danang isn't my home base, but I'll be beaucoup happy to light there. Out."

Danang was more than three hundred miles south of our position or about thirty-six minutes at Weasel 4's airspeed. About half the distance to Danang was over enemy waters, but would be much less a problem than Weasel 4 bailing out over land. After a second refueling, Weasel 4 landed his battered F-4G safely at Danang Air Base.

Billy, Steve, Edgar and I celebrated Memorial Day back home at K. I. Sawyer Air Force Base, Michigan. We were cold war warriors once again.

Chapter 10:
Real World Struggles

The greatest event of my life occurred in December 1972. Elaine Moses, a student at Northern Michigan University, and I were married at Rahway, New Jersey. Together, we looked forward to our next significant event–my separation from the Air Force scheduled for 13 November 1973, only eleven months hence.

During my last months at K. I. Sawyer Air Force Base, I was encouraged by the quickening pace of the drawdown of aircraft from the war in Vietnam. More and more pilots took the opportunity to separate from the Air Force and get jobs as commercial airline pilots. KC-135 pilots were especially good candidates for airlines that were hiring due to the similarities between the Boeing KC-135 cargo tanker and the Boeing 707 jetliner. My dream was of a bright new future for Elaine and me when a major Southern airline scheduled me for a class with other pilots to fly their large passenger aircraft.

Then, my dreams and Elaine's were dashed by another war.

Less than six weeks before I was to separate from the Air Force, Egypt and Syria launched a surprise attack on Israel on Yom Kippur, 6 October 1973. Three weeks later, the Yom Kippur War was over and I was short, but still in the Air Force. Upon learning from TV news that President Nixon had ordered the resupply of Israel, I wondered if KC-135 crews might be deployed to support the airlift–thus retaining me beyond my separation date. Two weeks after the Yom Kippur War ended, I was a civilian.

Little did I know that a meeting in Riyadh, Saudi Arabia two months before the war began would be my undoing. Egypt's President Anwar Sadat had met in the Saudi capital with King Faisal and the two had agreed on a plan to use oil as a weapon of war and negotiation leverage. In late October, the Saudi dominated Organization of the Petroleum Exporting Countries (OPEC) announced an oil embargo against the United States and other supporters of Israel. Soon, I learned what an oil embargo really meant. It hit home when I was turned away from a gasoline station after waiting in a long line of cars and told when I reached the pump that I could get no gasoline; but I could get ten gallons the next day because my license plate number ended in an odd digit. I thought *wow*!

As the days and weeks rolled by, I thought I understood the impact the embargo was having on everyday life and the economy in the United States. Wrong. Then, the hammer fell. Two weeks before my class was to begin, a letter arrived from the major airline on which I was counting. The letter announced the furlough of current pilots and the cancellation of my class for new pilots. Distraught, I read the letter several times before sharing the bad news with Elaine. "Honey, we've been dealt a tough hand."

Not only was my potential major airline furloughing pilots because of the fuel shortage; all major US airlines were doing the same. Nineteen percent of all US airline pilots were furloughed. In great anticipation, I had waited for the job at one of the majors. With that gone, I had no other job prospects or skills.

Then, I tried for a position in an Air Force Reserve unit flying KC-135s. No vacancies. All the KC-135 positions had been taken by ex-Air Force pilots furloughed by the airlines. I kept telling myself, *I'm a pilot and a damned good one. Now I'm in a jam. What can I do? How can I change my heading?*

Looking for work unrelated to my only skill felt like shooting in the dark until I remembered a friend in Detroit who had told me some years before that he would hire me if need be upon my departure from the Air Force. Besides, Detroit would put me close to my wife, Elaine, who was still at Northern Michigan University in Marquette, Michigan. In a desperate and fateful phone call, my friend offered me a job in middle management. He was the Operations Manager at McDonald's in Detroit. With a smile, I took the thirteen thousand dollar a year job, about half the pay of an Air Force captain on flight status with seven years' service.

* * *

My tour of duty at McDonald's began in a store. The store where I worked was not a franchise; it was corporate owned and called a McOpCo. There, I learned store operations, management skills, how to handle irate customers, and how to make burgers. I became known as "Speedy" because I made burgers so fast. Most essentially, I learned how to conduct the all-important nightly inventory. The next step up the ladder would be a McOpCo store manager, followed by area supervisor, then operations manager. An operations manager was responsible for a district that included several stores. From that position, I could eventually own a store.

McDonald's was not the career I had hoped for, but I was thankful for a job and I would play this new hand dealt to me. My life was on another unexpected heading. Nonetheless, I resolved to do my best work in my new job.

* * *

One night during closing, an unshaven inebriated man entered the store. He said, "Look here, sonny. I have business with the manager." Then he demanded in a menacing voice, "Send his ass on over here."

"Yes, sir!"

With the hair on my neck rising, I fetched the store manager.

When the manager was face to face with the drunken man, the man pulled out a gun and pointed it at the manager's head. "Gimme all the got damn money in every register and the safe. And be quick about it. I ain't got all fuckin' night."

The manager said to the employee standing next to me, "Empty the registers into a bag and bring it to me."

To the robber, he said, "Sir, I will give you all of the money in the registers. However, I cannot open the safe...."

The robber cut him off. "The hell you say. Open the muthafucka or die!"

"Sir, let me explain. This is a two-key safe. I have one key. The armored truck driver has the second key. Both keys are required to open the safe." The gunman looked confused. The manager hesitated, and then added, "Sir, if you wish, you can go out and get a crowbar. Then, I'll help you open it."

The robber paused, looking from one employee to another. And then he said to the manager, "Damn you, gimme dat bag o'money."

After a quick glance to see that there was actual money in the bag, the robber ran for the door. Near the door, he stumbled and fell. His gun discharged. I felt my heart pound. No one was injured. The robber recovered and ran out the door.

I exhaled. The relief I felt reminded me of escaping the burning C-47. I was shaking my head and thanking God.

The robber had not chosen to lock us in the freezer, or perhaps he forgot. Locking restaurant employees in the freezer was in vogue with robbers during the 1970s. The freezer in this store was preferable to the wrong end of a robber's gun, for an alarm device was installed in the freezer that we could use to alert the police. This was another bad hand and I was really ready for this game to be over. Then and there, I decided I needed a new heading.

Worse was my hurry to have a place of my own and end boarding in the home of another Madison homeboy, an electrical engineer named, Bobby Carter. I felt pressure that I put upon myself to limit my time of imposition on Bobby. In haste, I bought a twenty-year-old ranch house with a basement. I thought I was doing the right thing to establish a place for Elaine and me. Only later did I realize that I had made a colossal mistake. The enormity of my error in judgment came when I saw the look on Elaine's face the first time she saw the house. The pain in her face was greater than the reaction I saw when I told her the airline had cancelled my class. It was too late. I had completed the purchase without discussing the matter with her or offering her the opportunity to see the house before I closed the deal.

First, it was bad. Then it got worse. While I was working nights at McDonald's, Elaine reported hearing ghosts! She asked her grandmother to stay in the house with her. Both women declared they heard ghosts. It did not matter one whit, not one iota, in the few months we spent in the house that I could not hear ghosts. I had made an awful decision. No. It was not about buying a haunted house–it was worse. My big blunder was buying a house without my wife's participation! Tough lesson. Never again….

* * *

The OPEC oil embargo ended in March 1974. Two months later, Piedmont Airlines, a small regional carrier, invited me to North Carolina for an interview. I was hoping for a call from any major airline. At this point, I thought *it did not matter. Any flying job would be just fine.* But my strong preference remained: fly for a major.

* * *

One spring evening in 1974 after scrubbing the smell of hamburgers from my body, the phone rang. Elaine did not avert her eyes from the television as she said, "Your turn."

I lifted the receiver. "Hello."

"Hey, Carl. You'll never guess where I am!"

I laughed. "That's easy. Knowing you, C. J., it's got to be a bar."

"Okay, okay. Of course, you're right. But that's not what I mean."

"Well, explain yo'self, boy, before that liquor makes you forget yo' name."

When he controlled his laughter, C. J. interrupted me laughing at my joke. "I'm in a class for new pilots at Piedmont Airlines."

"What?"

"I know you heard me. I'm in a class for new pilots at Piedmont Airlines."

My old friend, C. J. Hayes, from KC-135 training days at Castle Air Force Base, California was out of the Air Force. C. J., a former B-52 pilot, and I had served together as well at U-Tapao Air Base in Thailand. He was also in my wedding party in 1972.

I sat. "C. J., what the fuck is Piedmont Airlines? Is it some country-ass crop dusting outfit? Where're you calling from anyway?"

"Piedmont is located in Winston-Salem, North Carolina. And they don't dust crops, smartass. Piedmont is a regional airline."

"Well, fuck me. I never heard of'em. Where do they fly?"

"In a word, the Southeast. Listen, cut the horseshit and lemme tell you why I called. I'm the second black pilot they've hired. And they're looking to hire more."

Finally, I'm curious. "How do you know they want more of us?"

"A senior pilot told me. That's how I know."

"No shit?"

"No shit. And he's interested in you."

"Huh? Me?"

"Yes, you, turkey. Now here's the thing. I went to see the chief pilot. He sat behind his desk leaning back in his chair and scratching his chin while I told him how I knew you. You know the usual stuff, experienced Air Force pilot with seven years of service, blah, blah, etc. Then, I told him about your heroics landing the burning C-47 and your Distinguished Flying Cross. He suddenly sat up straight. When I mentioned you were an aircraft commander flying the KC-135, his eyes went wide and he handed me his business card. Then he simply said, 'Tell your friend to fax me his resume.'"

C. J. couldn't know that by now my eyes were open wide, too. Then reluctance reared its head again and wishing for a call from a major returned. I sighed. "Eh, so, which airplanes do these people fly?"

"Wait a minute. What the fuck do you care?" C. J. paused. I could not think of a response. C. J. sighed and continued. "Anyway, they fly turboprops and jets. Say, are you suddenly getting cold feet? You told me you wanted a career flying airplanes, didn't you? What happen? Did you change yo' weak-ass mind?"

"Eh, yeah. Er, no. You know what I mean. But...."

"But nothing. Boy, get yo'ass in gear and send yo' shit in!"

"Okay, okay. Though, I never heard of this outfit, I'll consider them since you recommend this Piedmont. Give me his contact info."

* * *

After two busy days at the Mickey-D store, C. J. called again. "Now, look here Carl. Don't you embarrass me in front o' these white folks. Captain Tadlock stopped me in the hallway and told me he hasn't heard from you. He asked me, 'Does your friend know how many people want this job?' So I'm asking you, what the fuck? Over!"

I was at a loss for words. Finally, I said, "What'd you say they flew? And how many pilots do they have?"

"Dammit! I already told you what Piedmont flies. They have forty to fifty planes and more than four hundred pilots to fly'em."

"So less than ten percent...."

"Enough with the fuckin' numbers! Why are you stalling? It's just a job. If you don't want the job, say so. Talk to me. What's up?"

Sobered by C. J. exasperated tone, I said, "C. J., I want you to know that I really appreciate what you're doing for me."

"Well, show me by getting on with this thing! What the hell's holding you back?"

I tried to think of why I was reluctant as I stammered, "I-it-it must be.... It's just that I-I-I guess I'm still hoping for a call from a major airline. You know, one everybody's heard of."

I heard a long annoyed sigh. Then in a calm voice, C. J. said, "Carl, have you ever heard that a bird in hand...."

I cut C. J. off. "Yeah, yeah. ...Is worth two in the bush." I chastised myself for vainness and vagueness. I silently expressed gratitude for an opportunity that could be the better new heading I had prayed for. To C. J., I said, "Okay. I'll send my resume."

* * *

Captain Jack Tadlock, Chief Pilot and Vice-President of Flight Operations at Piedmont Airlines responded to my resume by sending a telegram inviting me to an interview at Piedmont's Winston-Salem headquarters. Reluctance returned. I was more than two hours late for the interview. I was directed to Captain Tadlock's office past a line of people outside of his office. The look on Captain Tadlock's face as I entered his office told me I might not get this job. He was clearly not happy with my late arrival. Suddenly, I realized deep within that I wanted this opportunity.

Tadlock removed his glasses and looked me up and down. He spoke in an even tone. "Son, do you want this job?"

Wide-eyed, I answered, "Yes, sir."

"You're interviewing for the last available pilot slot. Your late arrival for this interview does not demonstrate strong interest on your part. Are you really interested in flying for Piedmont?"

"Yes, sir."

Tadlock pointed toward his door. "Did you see that line of people out there?"

Maintaining eye contact, I said, "Yes, sir."

"Those people are pilots waiting to see who will get the offer for the last available pilot slot."

A cold shudder went down my spine causing me to shift in my seat. I thought *Damn, because of my unwarranted and stupid reluctance I may not get this job.*

"Captain Tadlock, sir, I'm very sorry about arriving late. Tardiness is unusual for me. But sir, if you hire me, it will not happen again. Sir, I want you to know that I will do whatever it takes to be one of the best pilots at Piedmont Airlines."

For a long moment, Tadlock's gaze into my eyes was steady. He did not blink or smile. I forced myself not to blink. I could feel him measure me. And then he looked down and held my resume in both hands. I waited in the silence that permeated the room while he reread my resume. Presently, Tadlock looked up. "Mr.

Gamble, based on your resume, I would hire you. But in our process, a second senior pilot interviews all candidates. He waited for you, but left for the day shortly after the time you should have arrived. Therefore, I will have to call you tomorrow and let you know if he agrees with me to hire you."

I spent a fretful and prayerful night at my sister Bobbie's house in Manassas, Virginia, waiting for Captain Tadlock to call with Piedmont's decision.

* * *

I am thankful and will always be grateful to C. J. for rescuing me from flipping burgers at Mickey D's.

On May 27, 1974, I reported for pilot training at Piedmont Airlines. Though I knew it was a small airline, I was still disappointed that I did not see the McDonnell Douglas DC-9s, Boeing 727s, or Lockheed L-1011s that my friends were flying at other airlines. Piedmont's only jets were several Boeing 737-200s.

I resigned myself to my new reality. During the probation period of one year, I would fly a small fifty-eight seat airplane for little more than half my annual salary at Mickey-D's. My first year salary at Piedmont was $7,500.

My first airplane at Piedmont was the twin-turboprop YS-11A-205. I was surprised to learn that the Japanese designed the YS-11 as a replacement for the Douglas DC-3s (remember my ancient C-47 in Vietnam) still in use on Japan's domestic air routes in the 1950s. The model 205 was developed specifically to meet the needs of Piedmont Airlines to lift a larger load from the small airports it served. The YS-11 seated six more passengers than Piedmont's other turboprop, the Fairchild FH-227 (Fokker F27). Its lift ability made the YS-11 the perfect "puddle jumper" for Piedmont. From my domicile base at DCA (Washington National Airport), I made seven stops en route to Atlanta in Richmond, VA, Rocky Mount, NC, Raleigh, NC, Charlotte, NC, Greenville-Spartanburg, SC, and Tri- Cities, TN.

On one memorable puddle jumping journey, an elderly European lady arrived at Washington National Airport via taxi from Washington's Dulles International Airport. Her European airline had flown her from London, United Kingdom and arranged the taxi for her onward travel on Piedmont Airlines to her destination at London, Kentucky. The lady's lack of understanding of spoken English rendered the public address system announcements made by flight attendants meaningless to her. At every stop, she attempted to deplane only to have a flight attendant return her to her seat. Upon finally arriving at the London, Kentucky airport, the exasperated lady declared in accented English, "Ze trip from Vashington to Kentucky took almos' as long as ze trip from Great Britain to Vashington. You people have made me very tired."

Low pay during the probation year and twelve-hour duty days of puddle jumping notwithstanding, pilots enjoyed an enviable lifestyle. One only needed to fly for twelve days per month. Eighteen days off felt like a monthly vacation. I know of no other industry where this was possible.

Elaine and I moved to Temple Hills, Maryland to be near Washington National Airport, just on the opposite side of the Potomac River. By now my nightmares were less frequent. Sometimes, in our new home, Elaine would wake me and let me know that I was whimpering in my sleep. She would hold my hands in the darkness and say, "See, your hands are fine. Your legs are not burned, either. There is no burning airplane. You're safe and at home with me."

At first, I commuted to Washington National Airport in my Corvette. That didn't last long. The reality set in quickly that the rent ($550) was almost as much as my salary ($600). To cope, Elaine got a job at the Pentagon and we sold my Corvette. We bought a Rabbit, a new car introduced in 1974 by Volkswagen for the 1975 model year to replace the Beetle. We ate well for the first half of each month, and then toward the end of the month, it was soup and cold cuts.

Plus, we had a dog to feed. Our dog, Rover, was a big mutt; a mix of Irish Setter and Collie. Since we could not afford dog food, Rover ate the same food we ate. Once, we arrived home from a movie one evening to find only scraps left from a loaf of sandwich bread. The hungry dog had removed the package from the table and ripped it asunder. That meant cold cuts without sandwich bread. Rover made other demonstrations of his disdain for us. Without damaging them, Rover removed my favorite Herbie Hancock LP album, "Head Hunters," from the album cover and placed a yellow sofa pillow in the middle of the floor. When he chewed and destroyed my favorite custom made-in-Vietnam jacket, Rover had to go.

Our real-world struggles meant I had to supplement my income. My second job paid more than Piedmont did during that probationary first year. In my second job, I earned twenty-five dollars for each person who responded to my sales pitch and visited vacation houses my employer was selling. With this additional income, some semblance of normalcy slowly arrived to our lives. At last, we could afford to buy the least expensive beverage when we hosted neighborhood house parties–Booth's Dry Gin, with the red lion on the label. In my stupor, I remember wondering why the lion posed with its left front paw raised while standing. That thought was quickly pushed aside as I joined Elaine and our neighbors in raucous laughter listening to Richard Pryor's LP album titled, "That Nigger's Crazy." We played the four-part album repeatedly. After more gin, Richard's lines about Dracula, the "Exorcist" and little green men from Mars landing in New York were funnier than they were an hour before. A house favorite was Richard's bit about the wino advising the junkie, which included the line, "Boy, dem muthafuckin' narcotics will make yo' lil' ugly ass null and void."

Amid the laughter, I was quiet at first during Richard's bit about the white police officer stopping a black motorist. I remembered the New Mexico officer who stopped me in my Corvette. Richard's motorist said, "Officer, I am *slo-o-owl-ly reachin-n-n'* into my pocket for my driver's license. I don't want no muthafuckin' accident happenin' 'round heah." Richard's album was released in 1974, only five years after my New Mexico police incident. At that 1974 party, I thought *what's changed between white policemen and black male motorists? Nothing's changed; not a damned thing.* As I write my memoir in 2016, I still think, not a damned thing's changed.

Music at our parties was limited. With Pryor's comedy, we played our Herbie Hancock album, and by December added a new album by Rufus featuring Chaka Kahn. Our house parties relieved the stress of limited funds for fun.

In August of the same tumultuous summer, across the Potomac River, Richard Nixon wrote on White House stationery a single sentence letter: "I hereby resign the Office of President of the United States." Gerald Ford got a new job. Meanwhile, Elaine and I slowly improved our lives with our three jobs.

My first full salary pilot's check arrived the following May. That was major welcome news. I was no longer a probationary new hire at Piedmont. Then another heading arrived by mail. In June, Piedmont furloughed me and many other pilots.

With my elbows on the kitchen table and my chin cupped in both hands, I said to Elaine, "Baby, this furlough makes it very clear why some of my Air Force buddies won't take a chance on the airlines. They still have their safe careers while I suddenly have zero pay." I sighed. "But that's neither here nor there. Let me get myself back to the matter at hand. What we need to do now is some figuring and make a new plan." While I was talking, Elaine went to the stereo and played the Rufus-Chaka Kahn hit, "Tell Me Something Good."

"Carl, sweetheart, by the time you finished reading Piedmont's letter to me, I figured out what the answer is. Move over so I can reach the phone. I'm calling Mama. There's nothing else to figure."

Shaking my head and feeling down and in the dumps, I had to smile. My wife, with accompanying music, had produced another of her positive thinking-no drama solutions.

We gave up our Temple Hills, Maryland condo and moved in with Elaine's parents in New Jersey–again.

* * *

A year passed before Piedmont called me back to fly again. In the meantime, I became a department store photographer in New Jersey.

I was anxious to fly again. My new flying domicile was Atlanta's Jackson-Hartsfield International Airport. Elaine and I made our new home in College Park, GA, just south and west of the airport. That did not last long. My second furlough came almost six months later. We moved in with Elaine's parents in New Jersey–again.

My second furlough ended a few months later and by March, Elaine and I moved again to Georgia. Our lives and those of Piedmont and sister airlines' employees were lived at the whim of Saudi Arabia and her OPEC cousins. While on furlough, friends flying with major airlines invited me to join them. I refused to leave Piedmont because the community of pilots felt like family. Our passengers were like a fan base. In a popular Piedmont practice, aircraft were usually named for a place served by Piedmont followed by the word *Pacemaker*; for example the *"Queen City Pacemaker"* honored Charlotte, North Carolina. The cities we served were extended kin. The leadership of Tom Davis, Piedmont's founder and CEO, and Chief Pilot Jack Tadlock felt comfortable. The furloughs were understandable. OPEC's control of the price and supply of fuel put a stranglehold on vulnerable airlines worldwide. I decided to stay put.

The next year, President Jimmy Carter signed the Airline Deregulation act of 1978 that gradually phased out the Civil Aeronautics Board and its rules governing details of airline operations down to the price of tickets and cities to serve. The same year marked the beginning of a soaring rise in "Speedbird," Piedmont's logo painted on the tail of its aircraft. Before the end of the Carter Presidency, Piedmont went into rapid expansion that included purchase of new jets and New York-based Empire Airlines. The fleet was nearly all jet by the end of the decade. In 1984, new 727-200s enabled Piedmont to fly from coast to coast, adding Los Angeles and Denver. The arrival of 737-300s a year later enabled flights to more western cities and as more time passed, Nassau and Bermuda international destinations were added. This meant the arrival of more and more new pilots on the seniority list below me, decreasing the likelihood that I would be furloughed again. While Jimmy Carter was still president, I was promoted to captain on the Boeing 737-200–unheard of advancement from first officer to captain in just six years compared to the usual twelve to eighteen years. In 1980, there were only a handful of black airline captains. I was very glad that I did not listen to my friends during the furlough and jump ship.

Airline captains reminded me of Air Force T-38 student pilots. Both thought of other pilots as lesser beings; probably put on Earth just to assist and laud their superiors–airline captains. I was no exception. Like my captain brethren, I took offense at the least slight. While I was beginning to feel comfortable that Piedmont's pilot seniority system insulated me from the kind of treatment I saw meted out to my Air Force friend, Lieutenant Colonel Joe Blaylock, I should have known that bigotry and racism lurked somewhere within Piedmont. I had certainly lived long enough to know. Yes, Piedmont was a part of the society it served and drew employees from that society.

On an otherwise bright and cheerful day, passengers had taken their seats and nearly filled my Boeing 737-200. Flight attendants were busy with last minute checks on the interior. We would soon be underway. Having completed my exterior inspection of the airplane, my copilot and I stood in the forward galley with a flight attendant when the gate agent boarded.

To my copilot, the gate agent extended papers and said, "Good morning, Captain. Here is your paperwork for this flight."

At first I was shocked. Then shock turned in to building anger. My copilot was embarrassed. While he was clearing his throat and changing colors, the flight attendant dropped her head and slipped away. I stood with my arms folded facing the agent. The copilot said, "Er, um, I'm not the captain." He pointed to me and said, "H-he is."

The agent turned toward me for the first time. I said, "You don't look like a new hire. In all my years with Piedmont Airlines, I've never seen a gate agent confuse a first officer with a captain. Did you not notice the three stripes on the copilot's epaulettes or the four on mine?" My hands slipped to akimbo. The agent flinched. I continued. "Or did you let the color of my skin help you illogically conclude that the white copilot on this flight must be the captain?" The agent's eyes grew wider. He handed me the papers and took a step back.

After a pause, I took a deep breath and resumed. "I'll tell you what. I don't need your lame-ass excuses." Louder, I said, "Get the hell off my airplane. Don't board any airplane on which I'm present." My anger grew. Louder still, I said, "You fathead muthafucka, get the hell outta my sight!"

As the gate agent left, the cabin crew and passengers were quiet. The agent reported me to his supervisor without explaining that he had provoked me. His supervisor passed the one-sided account on to the chief pilot. When I returned from my trip, the chief pilot was waiting for me. He listened to me in his office. When our chat was done, he said, "Carl, in the future, no matter your anger or how you're disrespected, I'll expect you to handle a situation like this with professionalism and aplomb–and out of the earshot of passengers."

"Yes, sir."

Chapter 11:
Piedmont Airlines Flight 451

At 3:20 p.m., a two-toned chime signaled an incoming call from a flight attendant. That was a surprise. I could not remember the last time a flight attendant called the cockpit when we were in final approach. My copilot and I exchanged a quick glance. I cannot remember the flight attendant's name, so I will call her, Anita. I said into the interphone, "This is Gamble, go ahead."

A nervous female voice just above a whisper said, "Captain, this is Anita on the aft phone. A man just handed me a note. We're being hijacked to Cuba."

I felt my eyes open wider and I tried to sit up straighter, but my harness held me in my seat. I exclaimed, "Huh? What did you say?"

"The note says that we're being hijacked to Cuba."

After a pause, I said, "Do you think this is a joke?"

"No, sir. He said he has two accomplices and they brought a bomb on board. The note says that if we don't go to Cuba they will detonate the bomb."

"Anita, hold the phone a sec." Upon hearing the word 'bomb', both my sphincter ani externus and sphincter pylori had slammed shut so hard that it felt like a blow to the back of my head. I shook my head violently trying to process what I just heard. The flash of adrenalin pumped in an instant through my body gave me the sensation of time travel back to Vietnam and into the cockpit of my burning C-47 in the same month fifteen years before. Though we were not on fire like my C-47 was, the threat was enough to demand action. However creditable the threat of harm to my passengers and airplane might be, I needed to respond and defuse the matter. I became determined not to allow Flight 451 to become a fireball. Fifty-seven passengers and my crew would perish. I thought, *Calm down, Carl. God, I need you.* Then I said to Ben Griffin, my copilot, "Squawk 7500."

Code 7500 was used by airline pilots to signal ATC (Air Traffic Control) that a hijacking was in progress. 7500 and various other codes were sent via the aircraft's transponder which was used to send digits by radio and identify aircraft on air traffic control radar. Transponders are not voice capable.

Ben's eyes went wide and I saw his chin drop as he stared at me. He said, "Huh?"

I said, "Yeah. Anita just read me a note from a damned hijacker."

"Damned is right."

"Go ahead and squawk 7500 now. Ask ATC for a racetrack so we can hold until I get this thing sorted out. Your airplane."

"Aye, Captain. My airplane. Squawking 7500."

Piedmont Airlines Flight 451 had originated at Newark's International Airport on Tuesday, March 27, 1984. My crew and I took over Flight 451, a Boeing 737-200, from the inbound crew at Charlotte Douglas International Airport and headed south. We made an intermediate stop in Charleston, SC and proceeded toward our final scheduled stop in Miami, FL. The weather was perfect for flying and our journey was routine–that is, until Anita called me during final approach into Miami International Airport.

Feeling sweat beads rising, I loosened my tie, unbuttoned my starched collar, and pointed the air nozzle directly at my face. During two deep breaths, I figured out what to do. Back on the phone, I said, "Anita, bring me the note. Tell this guy to wait for you at your station. Make sure he doesn't follow you."

* * *

Anita relocked the cockpit door after entering. After a quick scan of the note, I strained to remember a previous hijacking to Cuba. It had been awhile. Aloud, I said, "This could be a hoax. Well, maybe I'm hoping it's a hoax. It seems as if this hijacking mess was a '70s thing."

Ben said, "Yeah, it could be all bullshit. But you never know what kinda nut we have here."

While I was nodding in agreement with Ben and reading the note a second time, Anita said, "This guy seems calm and acts like a man with a purpose. I don't think this is a joke."

The note identified the hijacker as Lieutenant Spartacus of the Black Liberation Army. The two accomplices he claimed were not named. I read a third time the sentence threatening to detonate his bomb and blow my airplane out of the sky. I thought, *This shit is old but still chilling. Again, I asked myself: Didn't this 'hijack to Cuba thing' go out of fashion in the '70s along with robbers putting restaurant employees in the freezer?*

After a sigh, I said, "I'm leaning toward this is not a joke. Unless you guys have some other thought for me to consider, here's what we do." I paused. Ben and Anita waited in silence. I continued, "Anita, on your way back, quietly alert the crew. Have them scan the cabin and see if we can identify the accomplices of this Lieutenant Spartacus. While that's going on, call me and put Spartacus on the phone. Thoughts? Anyone?"

Ben said, "There isn't much else we can do."

I said, "Okay, Anita. Go."

"Yes, sir."

* * *

While rummaging through my flight bag, I asked, "Ben, do you have a map covering South Florida and Cuba?"

Ben glanced at me as I tossed map after map aside. "I dunno. Lemme go through my bag, too."

"Never mind. This might do." I studied two maps; one of which encompassed Miami and Key West while the second showed northwest Cuba, including Havana. After a minute, trying to ignore Ben's continuing yammering with ATC, I estimated that we had enough fuel to make a thirty-five-minute trek to Havana's José Marti International Airport without using our reserve.

Setting our second VHF radio to the frequency at Piedmont's Miami Operations, I said, "MIA OPS, this is 451 in a 7500 situation."

"Yeah, 451. ATC just passed that info to us."

"Here's our fuel on board." I read my gauges aloud and said, "Confirm sufficient to reach Havana without using reserve. When I call back after talking to the hijacker, patch me through to dispatch."

The interphone chimed. I said, "Anita, are you ready?"

"Yes, sir. I'm handing the phone to him."

A male voice with a thick accent said, "Hello."

"This is Captain Gamble. Sir, I read your note. Are you playing some kind of joke on us? If so, we can discuss this in full after we land in Miami. We can take care of any issues you may have after we're on the ground."

"Captain, I assure you, this is no joke. If you land this airplane in Miami instead of Havana, I will detonate this bomb and blow us out of the sky. Then the death of all these passengers will be on your hands."

My anger was rising. I decided to end the call. "Okay, Mister. See you on the ground."

Anita called back almost immediately, "Captain, we can't identify anyone for sure who may be accomplices. And, by the way, our 7500 has locked himself in the toilet."

"No matter. Thanks for trying."

As I switched back to VHF2, I said to Ben, "The bastard's locked himself in the toilet. Go ahead and execute your remote flush button and eject his ass."

We laughed together. Breaking the tension felt good. Ben said, "Sorry, Carl. But my damn flush button doesn't seem to work on this airplane."

"Too fuckin' bad."

Ben continued making left turns to keep us in orbit on our assigned racetrack over the Atlantic Ocean off Fort Lauderdale, Florida. For a fleeting moment, it reminded me of my long gone KC-135 days. I thought, *Life is not simple; no matter whether I'm in the military or out.* I rubbed my chin for a few seconds. Then I thought *I oughta give this thing at least one more shot....*

I rang Anita. "Let's try again. Go to the toilet door and ask Mr. Asshole again if we can't work this thing out in Miami. I'll stay on the phone."

"Yes, sir." I heard Anita move a few steps to the toilet door, knock softly, and speak to the hijacker. "Sir, the captain wants to know if we can work out your issues in Miami." There was a pause. I could not hear the hijacker's response. Anita spoke again. "Captain, he said his position has not changed; that if we land in Miami instead of Havana, he will detonate his bomb and blow up the airplane."

"Okay, Anita. Thanks for your help."

"Sir, I'm back at my station. What're you going to do?"

"We'll take the sombitch to Havana."

With a sigh, into the VHF2 radio I said, "MIA OPS, this is 451. Patch me through to Dispatch."

"Roger."

After a pause, I heard, "Hey, Carl. This is Dispatch. Go ahead."

"Hi, Dispatch. Our sonavabitch hijacker threatened, in a calm voice no less, to detonate his bomb if we don't take his sorry ass to Havana. Twice, he refused my overtures to work out matters in Miami. We have fifty-seven souls on board whose lives are in our hands. If you confirm that we have sufficient fuel, I need to get us on our way to Havana before we burn more fuel."

"Okay, Carl this is Dispatch. I'll make this quick. You have more than enough fuel. About the hijacker, I concur. Take his ass on to Cuba. We're on the same page. We went ahead and worked out a flight plan for you with ATC. Good luck."

"Thanks. Out."

Back on VHF1, I said, "ATC, this is 451. Do you have a flight plan for us?"

"This is ATC. Affirmative. Ready to copy?"

"Ready."

"MIA-J79-EYW-G765-HAV. Stay in the G765 corridor or Mr. Castro will scramble fighters up to meet you." I noted the flight plan and read it back.

I swallowed hard. I was making my first international flight since my Air Force days–and, I'm going into a hostile country. Suddenly, I could not think of anymore gallows humor. So, I said, "Roger. We're on our way."

"Roger. We'll have to arrange refueling with the Cubans by the time you arrive. Good luck."

"Thanks. Roger, out."

"Okay, Ben. My airplane."

"Aye. Your airplane."

Only about thirty-five minutes had elapsed since Anita's first call, but it seemed much more time had passed.

* * *

We made a slight left turn over Key West, Florida and entered the G765 corridor which led straight to Havana–235 air miles from Miami. Piedmont's policy was to serve no alcohol during emergencies. But I gave Anita and her crew permission to serve one drink per passenger. I thought that might help keep the passengers calm. Unbeknownst to me at the time, several passengers had overheard Lieutenant Spartacus and Anita on the phone. I learned later from a Miami newspaper that journalists had interviewed passengers after our return who knew we were going to Cuba and had made jokes about it.

In my best calm voice, I announced on the public address system, "Ladies and gentlemen, this is Captain Gamble. Due to complications beyond our control, we will make an unscheduled landing."

While still some distance from land, I heard on VHF1, "Buenas tardes, PI 451. Bienvenido a La Habana. This is Habana ATC. You are cleared to land on runway 24. Listen carefully to instructions...." We landed at 4:24 p.m. without incident on José Marti International Airport's single runway–nearly three miles long.

"PI 451, this is Habana ATC, again. Go all the way to the end of the runway and wait there."

"Roger."

Ben laughed. "I guess they wanna make sure if a bomb explodes, no Cubans will die."

At the end of the runway, I made a U-turn and parked our 737-200. The airplane was quickly surrounded by a Cuban security force of about fifty men equipped with carbines and handguns. They brought dogs to assist in their search for explosives. First, they allowed the passengers to disembark. The crew exited next. They waited for and arrested the hijacker. When all luggage had been removed from the cabin and the cargo bay, no explosives were found.

I shrugged and said to Ben, "That sombitch lied and got his trip to Cuba."

"Carl, there was nothing else you could've done."

With a sigh, I said, "Yeah. You're right. And I would do the same again to protect my passengers and crew."

"Now, I know how you earned your Distinguished Flying Cross. You're one cool dude when the shit hits the fan."

I felt embarrassed, so I changed the subject. "Thanks. Let's get the crew moving and round up the passengers. I'm ready to get on to Miami."

Anita laughed. "Good idea. If we start now, we may be able to pry them out of that duty-free shop by the time we're reloaded and refueled."

* * *

Climbing the truck-mounted stairs to reboard the airplane was a challenge for several passengers. In general, the lot of them seemed in a surprisingly jovial mood for hijack victims. I soon understood why they were a happy lot; some had already sampled the rum purchased in the terminal's duty-free shop. Many stumbled on the stairs, but they managed.

One exception was a woman wearing an expensive blue suit with white pinstripes and a white blouse sporting ruffles covering the buttons. She was carrying her navy-blue purse on one shoulder and two recently purchased packages. An early sign of trouble came when she wobbled, on her matching navy blue pumps, into the right side of the stairway on the first step. She tried to back off and start again. Her packages, including a half-consumed bottle of rum, shifted and sent her sprawling to the asphalt in an awkward position on her bottom, skirt askew. Anita and another flight attendant descended the stairs and each took an arm of the beleaguered, but happy, woman and helped her reboard. The woman smiled the whole time. A volunteer passenger ascended the stairs with the woman's packages.

The flight to the United States was one big half-hour party. We landed at Miami International Airport at 6:59 p.m. Upon arrival, cargo, luggage, and the airplane were examined again perchance a bomb had been placed aboard for our return trip. The crew was debriefed by representatives from the Federal Bureau of Investigation and the Federal Aviation Administration. Also on hand was Donald McGuire, who had flown in from Piedmont's Winston-Salem, NC headquarters to meet us and handle inquiries from the throng of reporters representing local and national news outlets.

Man, was I glad McGuire was there to keep the press off the crew. The receding adrenalin had left me tired and with a foreboding feeling, not too unlike my state in Vietnam after landing the burning C-47. I was even happier when McGuire announced that, to aid in unwinding; the crew could order anything we wanted at the hotel. I ordered a New York strip steak and Dom Perignon champagne. After the hijacking, my stomach was not in good shape. Alas, I could not eat the beautiful steak with grill patterns seared into its surface and covered with mushrooms and delicately sliced onions. But I managed to drink the champagne.

In a phone call, I told Elaine and our children that I was safe and how much I loved them. After calling a few disbelieving friends to tell them about the hijacking, I called an Atlanta neighbor, Alvon Johnson. Mr. Johnson was a Tuskegee Airman who graduated in 1945, too late to see combat in World War II. Mr. Johnson said, "Boy, you know you can lie. Yo' ass ain't been to no damn Cuba. But that's a good one. So I'ma hang up on you and go on back to sleep. You can call me tomorrow and tell me the truth."

I gave up trying to convince people that I had been hijacked. My last thought before sleep was *thank you, Lord, for a good outcome–again.*

(**Miami Herald**, July 17, 2014. William Potts Jr., a self-described black militant, aka: Lieutenant Spartacus, who hijacked a U.S. jetliner to Cuba 30 years ago, told Miami-based U.S. District Judge Michael Moore that he was no longer that "same person." Potts said that after serving 13 years in a Cuban prison and raising a family on the island for another 16 years, he finally surrendered to U. S. federal authorities. Moore sentenced Potts to 20 years in prison for hijacking the New York-to-Miami flight to Havana in 1984.)

Chapter 12:
Flying Big Birds

Before you can be a champion, you have to be a contender. It's the climbing that makes the man. Getting to the top is an extra reward. -- Robert Lipsyte, **The Contender**

"Sweetheart, you've gone silent on me." Elaine smiled and sipped her champagne. "A penny for your thoughts...."

Blinking, I returned from a corner of my mind where there played a video of Mama, Bobbie, and me in a Madison County, Alabama cotton field. My eyes were unfocused and the first thing I saw through the window after being dragged back into the present was the undeveloped yard of our new house in Matthews, North Carolina. An instant before, my thoughts had been hundreds of miles away in Northern Alabama. We had migrated in 1987 from Atlanta, Georgia to Charlotte, North Carolina as Charlotte grew into Piedmont Airlines' largest and most important hub. Flying from the Charlotte base, I would be able to spend more time with Elaine and our children and less time commuting from Atlanta for flights that I was assigned to fly out of Charlotte.

Matthews was an intriguing bedroom community south of Charlotte and an easy commute to Charlotte-Douglas International Airport. Construction had begun on our house the year before. That cold Thursday evening in January 1987, Elaine and I sat in front of the flickering flames in the family room fireplace and reminisced about the adventure of building a house and hope we'd not have to repeat the experience. We were confident that we had connected with a school system whose quality was enviable for our daughter, Leilana, and son, Davian.

Elaine's voice brought me back. I blinked again. Momentarily, I said, "Honey, I was remembering blessings and realizing dreams come true." I set my half-full champagne glass on the cocktail table and stretched.

Elaine shifted closer to me on the sofa and leaned her head against me as I put my arm about her shoulders. She said, "Well, I, too, have blessings for which I'm very grateful. High on my list is your rock head. As I've said many times, I'm so glad you didn't listen to me when we first met and I told you, 'don't go away mad, but do go away!'"

Though I had heard that remark countless times, I laughed.

Elaine continued. "Now, tell me about these blessings and dreams on your mind."

"I was a small ragamuffin…." I paused. "…when I was trying to help Mama pick cotton. From cotton picker to airline captain has been one helluva journey. And what I'm realizing is, it didn't come as a reward because of my small faith or as a reward for the trifling lil' good I ever did."

Again, I paused. Elaine sipped her champagne. When my pause grew, she said, "Well, come on out with it. What's the rest of your realization? Or, should I say, 'revelation'?"

"In one word: grace. Only by God's grace have we enjoyed the gifts that brought us to this day."

"Amen to that. But do go on. Name a few."

"For starters, there was my safe return from Vietnam. Then, we must always remember that there is risk in my industry. God has kept me safe and healthy. Without good health, I couldn't have continued as an airline pilot."

"Oh, you sound like an athlete, maybe like Jackie Robinson. Now there's a guy who definitely depended on good health to do his job."

At the mention of my favorite second baseman, I laughed. "Just as Jackie was, I am a contender because my skills and health are good. In fact, Jackie earned a championship ring. Though mine is to come, I'm still able to compete. In my thirteen years at Piedmont, I've seen pilots, even captains, wash out because they failed to pass that semiannual check ride you've heard me talk about. The result is the same for not passing the annual physical."

"Hmmm. I had not thought of skills and health side by side for pilots. And to think, I was only joking when I mentioned Jackie."

"Well, every new pilot doubtless has the same championship dream–become a captain on the largest bird flown by his or her airline. And, unlike Jackie's case, there are other reasons a pilot's dream could be shattered."

"Oh?"

"Yes. Even if Jackie had agreed to play for the Giants when the Dodgers attempted to trade him, he wouldn't have gone to the bottom of a seniority list and have to start all over as pilots do when they lose their job and get hired by another airline. Jackie and his teammates don't know from seniority or furlough and I'm sure the thought of their major league ball club going out of business never entered their heads.

"Speaking of going out of business, airlines do go out of business. But lil' ol' puddle jumpin' Piedmont has been very successful. I'm so glad I stayed. As you know, the same year I was hijacked, Piedmont was named the 'Airline of the Year.' Since then, Piedmont has grown at the fantastic rate of twenty-five percent a year.

"So, to have been a captain for seven years already; one of the few blacks, with the salary that helped us build this house, and have my dream job, actually a job that does not feel like work, are the matters that I was reflecting on and thanking God for."

"So, sweetie, what's next for us? What's your crystal ball saying?"

I laughed. "The damn thing is all cloudy. I think it's busted. But here's what I have my eye on." Though there was no one else in earshot, I lowered my voice. "Piedmont has won the authority to fly nonstop from Charlotte to London's Gatwick International Airport."

Elaine turned toward me wearing an incredulous expression. "Huh? Did you mean to say Charlotte?"

"I certainly did. We beat out the likes of American and TWA."

Her eyes were wide and she had an impish grin across her face. "What does that mean? Shopping at Harrods? How 'bout Selfridges?"

Smiling, I ignored her shopping questions. "First, it means lil' ol' Piedmont will need to acquire large wide body airplanes, like the new Boeing 767. Now, I don't want to be too optimistic, but soon, I think I could be flying as a captain on the '76'. I want to contend for a spot and fly big birds." Then, I lowered my voice close to a whisper. "I really want the challenge of flying the '76'. I heard it is very high tech and a great flying machine. Oh, and according to circulating rumors, a captain on this airplane can expect a huge bump in pay." Elaine sat up straight, handed me my glass, held her glass high, and with misty eyes said, "Here's to my hero. Carl, I'm so proud of you."

* * *

Due to Piedmont's extraordinary expansion and profitability, it became a sought after property by larger airlines competing to grow. When Piedmont was bought by USAir in 1987, it had about twenty-two hundred pilots. By the time USAir completed the acquisitions of Pacific Southwest Airlines and Piedmont Airlines in 1989, the combined three carriers, operating under the USAir banner, had more than six-thousand pilots. In addition to London, USAir began service to Frankfort and Paris. As an expanding international carrier, USAir changed its name to US

Airways and adopted a stylized United States flag as its logo plus a new color motif.

During this period of rapid change, a retired Air Force AWACS (Airborne Warning and Control System) pilot, named George Sledge, joined Piedmont in its last year of existence. (The AWACS airplane was based on the KC-135.) This was near the time that I qualified as a captain on the Boeing 757 and 767. We met by happenstance in the flight operations center at Charlotte-Douglas and soon became fast friends. Later, we learned that our homes were in adjacent neighborhoods. Our wives met and became friends.

On a chilly Friday night, December 15, 2000, Elaine and I drove the short distance through fog and rain to George and Cheryl's house for our weekly titanic bid whist battle of the sexes. For a time after arrival, Elaine was still heaping praise on Cheryl's Christmas decorations.

With a big grin, I interrupted and said, "Hey, George, tonight is the beginning of our new winnin' streak. How long do you think the streak oughta continue?"

George set four custom drinks on the table. "Oh, I don't know. Whata ya say, we let'em win one sometime, maybe the Friday 'fore Mother's Day."

Cheryl and Elaine clucked as they shook their heads. Cheryl said, "Oh, Elaine, ain't they just downright pitiful."

Elaine said, "Uh-huh. I think they oughta be worryin' 'bout the same whuppin' we been puttin' on'em throughout the fall and gonna run on through next summer!"

Laughing with Elaine, Cheryl said, "Don't you think we could let'em win just once for Father's Day?"

"Oh, hell no! Magnanimity ain't welcome here. Honey, show no mercy!"

Our foursome laughed together at the usual trash-talking we engaged in before, during, and after our games. Cheryl ripped the cellophane off a new deck of cards and it was game on.

Again, George and I lost–quickly. It was bad. So George asked me to do my special Atlanta Braves Chief Nocahoma dance around the table and cast a spell on the cards. No matter how often I did the dance, the result was the same–another humiliating defeat.

During the second game, George, who was flying as first officer on 757s and 767s, said, "Tell me about that behemoth you've been flying. Is it true that your colossal bird is heavier than the '76' and carries more passengers while using less fuel?"

"The short answer is yes. It would take until Christmas to give a balanced and nuanced answer that fairly describes these two big birds. It comes down to two things in my mind: 1. Age: the '76' flew ten years before the '333'. 2. Plain ol' subjectivity. Just as I'm told, beauty lies in the eye of the beholder. Same applies to comparing the '76' and the '333'."

"Do you mean like yoke vs. joystick?"

"Yep. Personal preference."

"I think you forgot number 3."

"So I don't deny that I'm forgetful–before or after several drinks."

Elaine laughed. "I can testify to that as fact!"

Laughing, I said, "Okay. So what did I forget?"

Grinning, George continued. "Number 3 is a number from the rumor mill: twenty-eight thousand."

I threw off a two of diamonds. Still grinning, George was looking at me instead of the two of diamonds. I said, "Heads up, dude! You're on VFR."

Cheryl said, "Shut your face, Carl Gamble! No talking across the board."

It was my turn to grin. "Yeah. The rumor is true. For this huge new state-of-the-art airplane, the company is paying selected captains three-hundred-twenty-eight dollars per hour to fly them."

"Still based on working just a couple of weeks per month?"

"Yep."

Elaine gave me a smiling glance and blinked.

George said, "Congratulations, my friend. Welcome to the big leagues where champion captains fly big birds."

* * *

On a bright summer day in 2002, I stood at the bulkhead in the first-class cabin of my A330-300 and thanked deplaning passengers at London's Gatwick International Airport for their patronage. A distinguished-looking couple paused in front of me. The tall man, wearing a heavy salt-and-pepper mustache, said, "Captain, this was a great flight. Thank you so much for bringing us home safely from America."

"You're welcome. I hope your stay in the U. S. was pleasant."

His female companion said, "Yes, it was, thank you. Sorry. But I'm amazed to learn that such a small man flew this very large airplane."

I had heard that remark countless times. My response was always the same. "You don't need size to fly this airplane. What matters is the gray matter."

Smiling broadly, she gave the usual final comment: "Very good, Captain."

Gone were the YS-11 and 737 days when I was disrespected by certain passengers and employees. Times had changed and most international travelers seemed different from the passengers of my puddle jumping era. Still, there were those who said nothing, but at first sight of me gave a "deer in headlights" look that morphed into the "other" look of "how the hell did you get to be captain on this airplane" or, "if I had known, I would have taken a different flight." But I had changed, too. I had learned to take the good with the bad and not lose my temper when it was "the bad."

In 2002, I was having the time of my life. I was living my dream flying the A330 to London, Frankfort, Paris, and Madrid. I gave thanks repeatedly for my fabulous job–a job that still did not feel like work. Plus, Elaine and I could travel for leisure to other cities during my two weeks off each month. My exhilarating life gave new meaning to the Temptations hit song, "Cloud Nine." While I savored the feeling of my feet barely touching the ground, my *superego* helped me keep my *id* in check.

Reflecting on what I had learned from Mama and my experiences, I began formulating a message to the young people I met. I thought, *The advice to youth, especially to young people of color, will be: don't let anyone tell you what you can't do. Believe in your dream, commit yourself, contend, work hard, and you can make it happen. Don't let your size or the color of your skin prevent you from reaching your goal. Becoming and remaining a contender is how I became a champion.*

Part Four : A New Heading

Carl's mother, Ora Gamble Langford, circa. 1944. *From Carl Gamble's private collection.*

Carl and his mother, Ora Gamble Langford, circa. 1994. *From Carl Gamble's private collection.*

First Lieutenant Carl Gamble and supersonic T-38 trainer, Laughlin AFB, TX, spring 1968. *From Carl Gamble's private collection.*

Elaine and Carl at their wedding in December 1972. *From Carl Gamble's private collection.*

Son, Davian, daughter, Leilana with Carl and Elaine in February 2003. *From Carl Gamble's private collection.*

Carl and his sister, Bobbie Gamble Hall, in February 2003. *From Carl Gamble's private collection.*

Carl and Elaine in February 2003. *From Carl Gamble's private collection.*

Nasif Majeed and Carl in February 2003. *From Carl Gamble's private collection.*

Brian "Bee" Settles, Carl, and Lloyd "Fig" Newton in February 2003. *From Carl Gamble's private collection.*

General (Retired) Lloyd W. "Fig" Newton in February 2003. *From Carl Gamble's private collection.*

Tuskegee Airman Alvon Johnson, Mary Johnson, and Carl in February 2003. *From Carl Gamble's private collection.*

Brenda Kyle, daughter of Bill Kyle, Carl, and former Chief Pilot, Piedmont
Airlines, Bill Kyle in February 2003. *From Carl Gamble's private
collection.*

Boeing 767 ice sculpture. *From Carl Gamble's private collection.*

Carl in the Airbus A330-300 captain's seat. Circa. 2002. *From Carl Gamble's private collection.*

Carl in the Airbus A330-300 captain's seat. Circa. 2002. *From Carl Gamble's private collection.*

Carl addressing attendees at his retirement party in February 2003.
From Carl Gamble's private collection.

Boyhood friend, Virgil Gilliam, and Carl in February 2003. *From Carl Gamble's private collection.*

Carl Gamble

The House of Representatives in the Commonwealth of Massachusetts salutes Carl upon retirement in February 2003. *From Carl Gamble's private collection.*

Aviation pioneers: (above) my homeboy, Retired Delta Captain Walt Harris native of Madison, Alabama and (below) my Charlotte neighbor, the late UPS Captain Cerea Beal, Jr. *From Carl Gamble's private collection.*

The **Distinguished Flying Cross** is a military decoration awarded to any member of the United States Armed Forces who distinguishes himself or herself in support of operations by "heroism or extraordinary achievement while participating in an aerial flight."

CITATION ACCOMPANYING THE DISTINGUSHED
FLYING CROSS
AWARDED TO CARL GAMBLE

"Captain Carl Gamble distinguished himself by extraordinary achievement while participating in connection with military operations against an opposing armed force near Da Nang Republic of Vietnam, on 1 March 1969. On that date, Captain Gamble was in command of an unarmed C-47 aircraft which was hit by hostile antiaircraft fire rupturing a fuel tank. Though his aircraft was in flames and an engine feathered he assessed the situation and determined to attempt a landing rather crash land or bail his crew out over hostile territory. Despite two inflight fuel explosions, and dense smoke in the cockpit Captain Gamble maneuvered the stricken aircraft to a safe landing. The courage and skill displayed by Captain Gamble were instrumental in saving the lives of his crew and preventing the total destruction of a valuable aircraft. The professional competence, aerial skill, and devotion to duty displayed by Captain reflect great credit upon himself and the United States Air Force."

The burning C-47D I landed was destroyed. This photo of a twin includes the left engine, which was burning, and the airplane's only exit. *Photo provided courtesy of Wikimedia Commons license.*

This C-47D is dropping propaganda leaflets. *Photo provided courtesy of Wikimedia Commons license.*

The USAF KC-135 shown above is refueling a small tactical aircraft. The similarity of the KC-135s I flew to their sister, the Boeing 707 airliner (below), sparked my interest in a career as a commercial pilot. *Photos provided courtesy of Wikimedia Commons license.*

A Piedmont 737-300 (foreground) and a 737-200 (background) arrive at New York's La Guardia Airport. I was the captain on a Piedmont 737-200 flight hijacked to Cuba. *Photo provided courtesy of Wikimedia Commons license.*

A highlight in my career was flying big birds as captain on the 767-ER pictured above at London's Gatwick International Airport. *Photo provided courtesy of Wikimedia Commons license.*

Chapter 13:
Tailspin

On the day of my great retirement party, my life on "Cloud Nine" abruptly halted.

A Federal Express agent rang our doorbell on Saturday morning, February 1, 2003, and handed a letter to me from the Pension Benefit Guaranty Corporation (PBGC). The letter, dated January 31, 2003, announced January 31st as the start date of the sixty-day notification period in which the US Airways pension plan for pilots would be terminated and taken over by the PBGC on April 1, 2003. I thought, *This letter is just for my information since my retirement date was January 5, 2003. Or is it?*

Elaine arrived in the foyer as the Federal Express truck departed. With her hands akimbo, she asked, "So what's the big news? Is it another retirement gift?"

Shaking my head, I scanned the letter again. Confused and with my brow furrowed after the second reading, I handed the letter to Elaine without comment. I thought, *Am I denying what the letter actually said? Did I derive the meaning I wanted? Am I lying to myself?* Suddenly, I felt nauseous.

At first, Elaine read holding the letter in both hands. All the while, her face morphed from jovial to something between confusion and annoyance, yet vaguely familiar. Then I remembered it was the look from Detroit when she first saw the haunted house I bought. Nearing the end of the letter, Elaine covered her mouth with one hand. She handed the letter to me. Searching my eyes with her brow creased, Elaine said, "Honey, what does this mean?"

Reading for a third time, I shrugged and said, "I'm not sure. At first, I thought it was an FYI or CYA kind of letter. But now, seeing that somebody thought it was important enough to send by Federal Express and I see the word 'terminate,' I've changed my mind." After a sigh, I continued. "I think this thing is ominous. I still don't know fully what it means. But I'll be on the phone with admin first thing Monday morning."

"What is this PBGC?"

"I don't know."

* * *

On Saturday evening, February 1, 2003, my retirement party was praised by many invitees as the best party they had ever attended. The band had appropriate music with performance that exceeded expectations. The band's art matched the grandeur of the ice sculpture of a Boeing 767 handmade for the festivities. Three hundred or so souls gathered in the ballroom of Charlotte's popular Adams Mark Hotel and helped me celebrate my major life milestone–retirement. They came from far and near and represented the phases of my life–from grade school to university, to war, to husband, to father, to airline captain.

From Madison, Alabama, my boyhood home, Virgil came and told stories about me that those assembled had never heard. Virgil even let it be known that as a kid, I started fights and would need help. Virgil and friends helped me and told me repeatedly, "Duck." Duck became my nickname in grade school. And, of course, Virgil was there with and for me throughout my youth and later during visits to Madison.

My Tennessee State, Air Force, and Vietnam phase was well symbolized by the presence of classmate Air Force General (Retired) Lloyd W. "Fig" Newton. Another who served in Vietnam with me was retired airline captain and author Brian "Bee" Settles.

One of the senior pilots who hired me at Piedmont Airlines, Bill Kyle, and his daughter, Brenda, represented another phase of my life. The US Airways years included my friend George Sledge and many pilot and nonpilot employees who came to wish me well.

On my list of unforgettable events, my retirement party ranked right behind my wedding to Elaine. Graduation from Air Force Undergraduate Pilot Training was pushed down to third.

* * *

During my retirement party, I tried to remain jovial. Mostly, I succeeded. Inside, I slowly realized the PBGC letter meant a new heading was set for my life–and without my consent. As the hours ticked by on Sunday, the words "notification to terminate" reverberated in my head, causing physical pain.

Early Monday, I phoned US Airways' administrative offices and found a pleasant person who knew of the letter sent to me. After I asked several questions, she said, "Sir, I've told you all I know."

"Okay. Please tell me again, the bottom line is what?"

"The bottom line, sir, is all lump-sum pension payouts have been frozen. It's not just yours. The freeze affects every eligible retiree."

"Is that also true for vacation pay?"

"No, sir. Your vacation pay will be forthcoming."

My headache grew worse as I put the phone down. I thought, *Bad heading; curveball....*

* * *

After a bit of digging and talking to several recently retired pilots, I learned that the Pension Benefit Guaranty Corporation (PBGC) is an independent agency of the United States government created by the Employee Retirement Income Security Act of 1974 (ERISA). That did not mean much too me. Then I found that Congress created the PBGC to "encourage" the continuation and maintenance of voluntary private *defined benefit pension* plans. I nodded. Yes. That was US Airways' pilot's pension plan. Since filing Chapter 11 bankruptcy the previous August, the company had gotten permission from the Master Executive Committee of the pilot's union and a bankruptcy judge to terminate our plan and leave it to the PBGC to pay US Airways retired pilots a fraction of what the plan would have paid. The PBGC could only pay pension benefits up to a maximum guaranteed benefit set by law for participants who retire at 65.

Pilots had to retire at age 60. According to that January 31st letter, the first PBGC annuity check, a fraction of my expected pension, would arrive April 1st. I thought, *Damn, another curveball.*

The windfall that US Airways gained by unloading the pilot's pension fund removed a major debt from its books and that action made the company attractive to lenders and investors. Now US Airways could emerge from bankruptcy on March 31, 2003. The timing was perfect–exactly sixty days after the PBGC termination announcement letter.

* * *

For four days, I had been nonstop on the phone with my attorney and several of twenty-one other retiring US Airways pilots. As a group, we hired an attorney and sued US Airways over ending our *defined benefit plan* (pilot's pension plan). While litigation continued, US Airways refused to make any payments to us from our *defined contribution plan* (401k funds). *Humph. Another curveball. Where is the fastball I can hit out of the park?*

During four days of exile, mostly in one room at home, I had not showered, shaved, or brushed my teeth. My head was reeling as I tried to make sense of what had happened so quickly to the future I had planned for my family. I thought, *Thank God for Elaine's mortgage business. She can keep us afloat until I receive my 401k money and vacation pay from US Airways and finally the annuity payments begin from the PBGC.*

Now Elaine was furious with me and let me know she did not like my foul mood and worse, my foul body odors. She said, "I know this is a horrible thing they have done to you after twenty-nine years of faithful service. But you have to fight instead of feeling sorry for yourself." Elaine paused and sat before me. "I know you can fight. You have faced challenges before. And like before, you have to be strong. Now, pick yourself up and show'em what you're made of. I know that's what Mama Ora would tell you if she were alive today. It's not even like you to feel sorry for yourself."

Then she softened her tone. "I know this has been a devastating blow. But we'll be okay. Stick with your gang of twenty-one in the suit against US Airways. Go ahead and join the big group in the other litigation against the PBGC because of the way it is reducing everybody's pension. Use every means necessary to make it right."

All the while Elaine spoke; I sat with my head in my hands. When she finished, I thought, *She's right. I've been a fighter all my life. Best get on with contending. Contenders have to stay in shape. First, agenda item: shower.*

* * *

The effect of the PBGC's calculations on my pension was more egregious compared to many others. First, the PBGC rolled my retirement date back from 2003 to 2000. My pension would be based on the period before the years of my highest earnings–when I flew the A330 in 2001 and 2002. Then, after the rollback, their formula cut the reduced base. *Damn. Two more curveballs!*

In November 2003, our gang of twenty-two and US Airways settled the suit and payments from our defined benefit plan began. From the settlement, I got far less than the amount in my account on January 5, 2003–my retirement date. This was compounded by a new US Airways stock issued when the company emerged from bankruptcy March 31, 2003. The new stock was worth pennies on the dollar compared to the old stock. My problem was that my defined contribution (401k) funds were heavily invested in US Airways stock. *Curveball in the dirt.*

After retirement and the PBGC debacle, my nightmares of the burning airplane became more frequent and with new intensity. Elaine, as always, was there to reassure me after each occurrence. Again and again, she would hold my hands and tell me that my hands were okay. Eighteen months after retirement, I was diagnosed with Post Traumatic Stress Disorder and after suffering for years, effective medication was prescribed. Uncle George was right; some unseen scars of war remain for life.

I joined the larger group of pilots in the suit against the PBGC. That litigation dragged on for eleven years. The suit ended when the United States Supreme Court refused to hear our claims against the PBGC. *Damn. More curveballs. Game over.*

The Dallas Morning News: "In a decision released Monday, [June 30, 2014,] the US Supreme

Court declined to review a case in which US Airways pilots were challenging the Pension Benefit Guaranty Corp.'s calculation of their benefits."

When an airplane loses lift and behaves like a falling bowling ball, it is called an aeronautical stall. This predicament might more appropriately be called "dead in the water." I was dead in the water.

Chapter 14:
Level Flight

"From everyone who has been given much, much will be demanded...."
Jesus in Luke 12:48b, KIV Bible

"There is a debt of service due from every man to his country,
proportioned to the bounties which nature and fortune have
measured to him." **Thomas Jefferson** to Edward Rutledge, 1796.

"My fellow Americans, ask not what your country can do for you, ask what you can do for your country."
John F. Kennedy, 1961

Looking back at my life has made me a witness. One can say, "I did it my way." But, in my journey, "my way" was paved with help from a strong support system; people such as Mama who believed in me and encouraged me to believe in myself. She was my veritable rock from the beginning. I was very fortunate to have my mother's support and guidance. I regret that Mama did not live long enough to see me retire.

Sages, old and young, whose observations on life through different lenses from mine opened windows of opportunity or sometimes created epiphanies. Examples of good fortune came in the person of a young Air Force medical technician who was not obliged to help me. Without him, there would have been no Air Force career or glowing resume for senior Captains Tadlock and Kyle at Piedmont to believe in. Yes, I did it my way. But I want to make it clear that I realize now that good fortune and the good people who believed in me made a major difference and contributed much to my success.

My contributions were intertwined with the support systems in my life. Mama saw worth in me. So did Elaine Moses. Elaine stood with me through thick and thin–and believe me, there were plenty of thin times.

Aviation instructors at Tennessee State and employers gave noteworthy support. Their backing was evident in my promotions to captain and aircraft commander in the Air Force, and to captain at Piedmont Airlines. Finally, advancement to the elite position of captain of the largest and most prestigious airplane in the US Airways fleet (A330-300) meant that my contributions proved my mettle.

After a bumpy start, self-discipline kept me focused on my goal. Hard work resulted in honed skills that later enabled self-empowerment. The combination of my contributions and my support system was inextricable. I thank God for the supporting people He put in my life.

The years have taught me to take the bad with the good. Times came and passed when life did not seem fair–or good for that matter, especially with the financial curveballs thrown my way. My ordeals tempered, annealed, and molded me. Incidents with abusive passengers or in particular, disrespect from a fellow employee also served to shape me. This was principally true when I did not respond with the calm that had pervaded my decision making in a burning military airplane or a hijacked airliner. On the other hand, positive feedback came from both Air Force and airline colleagues as well as passengers that affirmed my leadership and skills. My realizations about dealing with the good and bad of life took time, and in time became another pillar in the foundation upon which my success was built.

As in Frank Sinatra's song, I have faced my last curtain call. My flying career is over. I haven't flown an airplane since I retired in 2003. Life in my America has given me much; my blue yonder and more. I see what is required of me now. Despite the devastating blow given me at the end when US Airways ended my pension plan and my tremendous anger that followed, I stand just a bit tarnished, but in armor that still shines. I am grateful to still stand–dignity intact.

Today, I am on a new heading and in level flight. My new priority is sharing my experiences and aviation knowledge with young people–especially youth of color. My purpose is to encourage and make youth aware of extraordinary careers in aviation. And for youth who are in need of a poke or a prod to help them realize the best in themselves, I am ready to go wherever in the world I am needed to advise and encourage.

Index